THE ATONEMENT

Loraine Boettner

GLH Publishing
Louisville, KY

Originally Published in 1941.
Copyright unrenewed, Public Domain

GLH Publishing Reprint, 2019
Note: An additional footnote has been added to quote that was previously unidentified.

ISBN:
  Paperback 978-1-948648-75-2
  Epub 978-1-948648-76-9

*Sign up for updates from GLH Publishing
using the link below and receive a free ebook.*
http://eepurl.com/gj9V19

CONTENTS

I. The Atonement 1

II. The Significance of Christ's Death 11

III. The Satisfaction View of the Atonement 24

IV. The Active and Passive Obedience of Christ .. 44

V. Christ As Our Ransomer 57

VI. The Representative Principle 62

VII. The Extent of the Atonement 70

VIII. Old Testament Ritual and Symbolism 87

IX. Erroneous Theories of the Atonement 105

I. THE ATONEMENT

The two great objectives to be accomplished by Jesus Christ in His mission to this world were, first, the removal of the curse under which mankind labored as a result of the disobedience and fall, and second, the restoration of men to the image and fellowship of God. Both of these were essential to salvation. The work of Christ in reconciling God and men we call the Atonement; and this doctrine, we believe, lies at the very heart of the Christian system.

In the nature of the case we are altogether dependent on Scripture for our knowledge concerning this doctrine and can know only what God has seen fit to reveal concerning it. Human philosophy and speculation can contribute practically nothing toward its solution, and should be held in abeyance. Our present purpose is to give a systematized account of what the Scriptures teach concerning it, and to show that this fits in perfectly with the longings and aspirations of an enlightened spiritual nature.

In one of Paul's most condensed statements of Christian truth we read: "For I delivered unto you first of all that which also I received: that Christ died for our sins according to the Scriptures; and that He was buried; and that He hath been raised on the third day according to the Scriptures," 1 Cor. 15:3. In this statement first place is given to the death of Christ. "Christ died for our sins" was the fundamental fact of the early Christian message, the cornerstone of its faith. But as soon as this simple fact is stated a number of vital questions are bound to arise. In order that we may have an intelligent understanding of this vital truth it is necessary that we know precisely what it was that Christ accomplished on the cross and how He did it. We cannot rest content with teaching that leaves the central doctrine of our faith shrouded in mystery and uncertainty. This does not mean that all mystery can be removed. But the Scriptures do supply the interpretation of the death of Christ that the inquiring mind legitimately asks for, and the salient factors concerning it should be known by all Christian people. Believing that the Bible is God's word to man, and that the statements of Scripture regarding the death of Christ were meant to be understood by ordinary Christian men and women, we shall not be deterred from this study by those who deprecate any "theory of the atonement." Rather we hold it to be our task and privilege under the promised guidance of the Holy Spirit to "search the Scriptures" until we reach that understanding which satisfies the mind and heart and conscience, and leads to certainty and finality.

We cannot expect to give a full explanation of the Atonement any more than we can give a full explanation of the nature of electricity, or of the force of gravity, or of our own mental and physical processes. But the main outlines of the plan of salvation are clearly revealed in the Scriptures, and it is both our privilege and our duty to acquaint ourselves with as much of that plan as God has seen fit to reveal. We are told, for instance, in broad terms that we are members of a fallen race, that God has given His only-begotten Son for our redemption, and that salvation is through Him and not through any works which we ourselves are able to do. Certainly anyone who accepts these facts and acts upon them will be saved. Yet, accepting these facts and acting upon them would appear to represent only a minimum of faith, and God has made it possible for us greatly to enrich and expand our knowledge of the way of salvation if we will but give careful attention to His word.

By way of background for this subject we are to remember that after God had created man He established certain moral laws by which man was to be governed, and solemnly announced that disobedience to these laws would bring an awful punishment. As a pure test of obedience man was given permission to eat of every tree of the garden except of the tree of the knowledge of good and evil. In regard to that tree he was told: "In the day that thou eatest thereof thou shalt surely die." But man deliberately and defiantly disobeyed that command. Through that disobedience he not only corrupted his moral nature, but made necessary the infliction of the prescribed penalty. In view of God's previously expressed good will toward man, the large degree of liberty granted to him, and his full knowledge of the consequences, this disobedience was especially heinous; because through it man in effect transferred his allegiance from God to the Devil.

Moreover, by his fall Adam corrupted not only himself but all of his posterity, since by divine appointment in this test he acted as their federal head and representative. Had man been left to suffer the penalty alone, he would have experienced not only physical death, but spiritual death as well, which means eternal separation from God and therefore endless progress in sin and suffering. Like the Devil and the demons, who also are fallen creatures and who have been abandoned to their fate, man was morally polluted and guilty and had neither the desire nor the ability to reform himself. Furthermore, it is very evident that no member of this fallen race was capable of paying the debt owed by any other, since each one was preoccupied with his own sin. Even if it had been possible to have found a truly righteous man who was also willing to bear the penalty for others, he could at most have delivered but one other person since he himself was only a man. Nowhere outside the Trinity was there a person either capable or willing to take the place of another, no one capable of suffering and dying, the one for the many. Nor had man the slightest grounds on which to base a request that he be excused from the penalty of the law. Hence his condition was truly desperate.

But fortunately for man there was One both able and willing to perform that service. It was for this purpose that the Lord Jesus Christ, the second Person of the Trinity, became incarnate and performed for man a double service, discharging, on the one hand, the penalty through His own suffering and death, and on the other, restoring to man holiness and life through His perfect obedience to the moral law. Thus was redeemed a multitude which no man can number. How appropriate, then, the words of Peter, "Ye were redeemed, not with corruptible things, with silver or gold, from your vain manner of life handed down from your fathers; but with precious blood, as of a lamb without blemish and without spot, even the blood of Christ," 1 Peter 1:18, 19. And how appropriate the words of the heavenly songs, "Worthy art thou to take the book, and to open the seals thereof: for thou wast slain, and didst purchase unto God with thy blood men of every tribe, and tongue, and people, and nation, and madest them to be unto our God a kingdom and priests; and they reign upon the earth," Rev. 5:9, 10; "Blessing, and glory, and wisdom, and thanksgiving, and honor, and power, and might, be unto our God for ever and ever," Rev. 7:12; "Great and marvellous are thy works, O Lord God, the Almighty; righteous and true are thy ways, thou King of the ages. Who shall not fear, O Lord, and glorify thy name? for thou only art holy; for all the nations shall come and worship before thee; for thy righteous acts have been made manifest," Rev. 15:3, 4.

The Infinite Value of Christ's Sacrifice

The chief mystery in regard to the Atonement appears to lie in the fact that God chooses to accept the unmerited sufferings of Christ as a just equivalent for the suffering due to sinners. The question then arises, How can the suffering of an innocent person be set to the account of a guilty person in such a way that the guilty person is freed from the obligation to suffer? Or, to state the question more specifically, How can the suffering which was endured by Christ be set to the credit of His people, and how can that suffering suffice to save the millions of mankind, or even all of the people of the world if they would but trust Him? Or again, as it is sometimes asked although somewhat erroneously, How can God, the first person, take the sin of a guilty man, the second person, and lay it on Christ, an innocent third person?

That this last form of the question does not state the case correctly is quite evident; and here we get at the heart of the matter. For when God, the first person, takes the sin of a guilty man, a second person, and lays it on Christ, He lays it not on a third person but on Himself. There is no third person in this transaction, because Christ is God, Deity incarnate. This last consideration many people fail to keep in mind, and their failure to do so is oftentimes the reason for their rejection of the whole Christian system, which then is, of course, made to appear fantastic, unreal, unjust. If God had taken the sin of one man and laid it on another mere man, that would indeed have been a flagrant violation of justice as the Unitarians and Modernists charge.

In view of the fact that Christ is God, and therefore a Person of infinite value and dignity, we have no hesitation in saying that the crucifixion of Christ was not only the world's worst crime, but that it was *a worse crime than that which would have been committed if the entire human race had been crucified*. Isaiah tells us that in comparison with man God is so great that even "the nations are as a drop in a bucket, and are accounted as the small dust of the balance," 40:15. Christ's Deity and creatorship is set forth by John when he says, "In the beginning was the Word, and the Word was with God, and the Word was God...All things were made through Him; and without Him was not anything made that hath been made...He was in the world, and the world was made through Him, and the world knew Him not," 1:1, 3, 10. Paul declares that "God was in Christ reconciling the world unto Himself," 2 Cor. 5:19; and in another place adds, "In Him were all things created, in the heavens and upon the earth, things visible and things invisible, whether thrones or dominions or principalities or powers; all things have been created through Him, and unto Him; and He is before all things, and in Him all things consist," Col. 1:16, 17. Even the first chapter of Genesis, which gives an account of the original creation, declares this same truth; for when read in the light of the New Testament we see that it was counsel within the Trinity when it was said, "Let us make man in our image." Paul states this same general truth in even more graphic words when he declares that the rulers of this world "crucified the Lord of glory," 1 Cor. 2:8, and when he refers to "the Church of the Lord" (the King James Version reads, "the Church of God") "which He purchased with His own blood," Acts 20:28. For sinful man thus to crucify his God was an infinitely heinous crime. Whatever may be said about the Atonement, it certainly cannot be said that the debt paid by Christ was of lesser value than that which would have been paid if all of those for whom He died had been left to suffer their own penalty.

In order to illustrate a little more clearly the infinite value of Christ's atonement we should like to use a very simple illustration. Doubtless all of us, for instance, have killed thousands of insects such as ants, beetles, grasshoppers. Perhaps we have even killed millions of them if we have plowed a field or set a large brush fire. Or perhaps we have killed a considerable number of birds or animals, either for food or because they had become pests. Yet we suffer no accusing conscience. But if we kill just one man we do have an accusing conscience which condemns us bitterly; for in that case we have committed *murder*. Even if we could imagine a whole world full of insects or animals and if we could kill them all at one stroke, we would have no accusing conscience. The reason for this difference is that man was created in the image of God, and is therefore of infinitely greater value than the insects or animals. Now in a manner similar to this, Christ, who was God incarnate, was not only of greater value than a man but was of greater value than the sum total of all men; and therefore the value of His suffering and death was amply sufficient to redeem as many of the human race as God sees fit to call to Himself. Christ did not, of course, suffer eternally as men would have done, nor was His pain as great as the sum total of that which would have fallen on man; but because He was a Person of infinite value and dignity His suffering was what God considered a just equivalent for that which was due to all of those who were to be redeemed.

And as we who have been redeemed read that awful account of the crucifixion let us remember that we had a part in it, that it was for our sin and as our Substitute that He suffered and died, regardless of whether or not we personally clamored for His death or drove the nails.

In order for us to understand how it was possible for Christ to have accomplished this work of redemption it is necessary for us to keep in mind the fact that He possessed two natures, one Divine and the other human, and that it was in His human nature that He suffered on the cross. But in our own persons—which are composed of two natures in vital union, the spiritual and the physical—whatever can be affirmed of either of our natures can be affirmed of us as persons. If a certain man is good, or if he is a keen thinker, or happy, or sorrowful, we say that he as a person is good, intellectual, happy, or sorrowful. If his body weighs one hundred and fifty pounds, or if he suffers a broken leg, or is sick, we say that that that person weighs that amount or suffers those things. Our spiritual nature is the more important, more dominant and controlling; yet what happens to either of our natures happens to us as persons. In a similar manner, Christ's Divine nature was the more important, more dominant and controlling; but since the two natures were vitally united what He experienced in either He experienced as a Person. Hence His suffering on the cross was God's suffering, and His death was in a real sense God's death for His people. This means that the death of Christ, through which the Atonement was accomplished, was a stupendous event; the most important event in the history of the universe, the central event in all history.

That an atonement of some kind was necessary if human beings were to be pardoned is very evident. The justice of God demands that sin shall be punished as definitely as it demands that righteousness shall be rewarded. God would not be just if He failed to do either. Consequently, the law which was set forth in the beginning, that the punishment for sin should be death—involving, of course, not only destruction of the body, but eternal separation of the spirit from God—could not simply be brushed aside or nullified. The honor and holiness of God were at stake, and when man sinned the penalty had to be paid. The idea of vicarious suffering underlay the entire sacrificial system of the Jews, impressing upon them the fact that a righteous God could make no compromise with sin, and that sin must be and eventually would be punished with its merited recompense, death.

In the Incarnation human nature is taken, as it were, into the very bosom of Deity, and is thus accorded an honor far above that given to angels. Although Christ's work of Atonement is completed, He still retains His resurrection body and will retain it forever; and thus will be exhibited one of the strongest possible evidences of God's unity with man and His measureless love for man.

No Injustice Done When Our Penalty Was Laid on Christ

Unitarians and Modernists sometimes object to this doctrine on the grounds that it is unjust to punish one person for the sins of another, and assert that the idea of vicarious suffering is abhorrent. We reply that there can be no injustice or impropriety connected with it when the person who suffers is the same one who, having made the law that such and such an offense should be followed by such and such a penalty and himself actuated by love and mercy, steps in and receives the penalty in his own person while at the same time he makes provision for the reformation of the offender. In financial matters we readily see that there is no injustice when a creditor remits a debt, provided that he assumes the loss himself. Now what God has done in the sphere of redemption is strictly parallel to this. He has assumed the loss Himself and has set us free. In this case God, who is the offended party, took the initiative and (1) permitted a substitution, (2) provided a substitute, and (3) substituted Himself. If after man fell, God, as the sovereign Ruler of the universe and with the purpose of manifesting His attributes of love and mercy before men and angels throughout eternal ages, voluntarily chose to pay man's debt, surely there are no grounds for objecting that such action was not right. And this, Paul tells us, is precisely what God has done: "God, being rich in mercy, for His great love wherewith He loved us, even when we were dead through our trespasses, made us alive together with Christ (by grace have ye been saved), and raised us up with Him, and made us to sit with Him in the heavenly places, in Christ Jesus: that in the ages to come He might show the exceeding riches of His grace in kindness toward us in Christ Jesus: for by grace have ye been saved through faith; and that not of yourselves, it is the gift of God," Eph. 2:4-9. The work of redemption, including its purpose, method and result, could hardly be stated in clearer language than this.

But it is small wonder that the Unitarians and Modernists object to the Christian doctrine of the Atonement. Since they see in Jesus only a man the Atonement can be, from their point of view, nothing but a colossal travesty, an insult to man's intelligence and to God. Unless Christ was both Divine and human, the whole Christian system is reduced to foolishness. Had Christ been only a man He no more could have saved others than could Stephen, or Huss, or Lincoln, or any other martyr. God cannot take the sins of a criminal and lay them on a good man, but He can take them and lay them on Himself; and that is what the doctrine of the Atonement teaches us that He has done.

II. The Significance of Christ's Death

If we compare the manner in which the service of the world's greatest men have been rendered, and that in which Christ's work of redemption was rendered, we are immediately impressed with an outstanding contrast. While the service of men is rendered during their lifetime, and while Christ too, for that matter, lived a life of unparalleled service, the climax of His work came at its very close, and our salvation is ascribed pre-eminently to His suffering and death. Practically all of the material recorded in the Gospels has to do with the events which occurred during the last three years of His life, and approximately one-third of the material has to do with the events of the last week, commonly known as Passion Week. The prominence thus given to the closing scenes indicates very clearly that the distinctive work of our Lord was accomplished not by His life but by His death. Neither His example nor His teaching reveals the love and mercy and justice of God so convincingly as does His death; and consequently the cross has become *par excellence* the Christian symbol.

During the latter part of the public ministry Jesus spoke repeatedly and insistently of the death which He was to suffer at Jerusalem. "From that time," says Matthew, marking the beginning of a period, "began Jesus to show unto His disciples, that He must go unto Jerusalem, and suffer many things of the elders and chief priests and scribes, and be killed," 16:21. "He took unto Him the twelve," says Luke, "and said unto them, Behold, we go up to Jerusalem, and all the things that are written through the prophets shall be accomplished unto the Son of man. For He shall be delivered up unto the Gentiles, and shall be mocked, and shamefully treated, and spit upon: and they shall scourge and kill Him," 18:31-33. When Moses and Elijah appeared in glory at the time of the Transfiguration they talked with Jesus concerning "His decease which He was about to accomplish at Jerusalem," Luke 9:31. We are told that when the time drew near that He should be received up "He steadfastly set His face to go to Jerusalem," Luke 9:51, knowing full well what awaited Him there. With such majestic determination did He press forward toward the cross that the disciples were "amazed" and "afraid," Mark 10:32. "I have a baptism to be baptized with; and how am I straightened till it be accomplished," He said to the disciples, Luke 12:50. Loving His people with an infinite love, and having come to earth specifically for their redemption, He longed to suffer and to accomplish His appointed work. In these and numerous other statements He shows His preoccupation with His death, and that in such a manner as to make clear that in His mind it constituted the most significant part of His work.

That the specific purpose of Christ's death was to secure forgiveness for others is taught directly in Scripture. "This is my blood of the covenant, which is poured out for many unto remission of sins," said He as He instituted the Lord's Supper which through all succeeding generations was to be observed as a memorial of His death, Matt. 26:28. "The Son of man came not to be ministered unto, but to minister, and to give His life a ransom for many," Mark 10:45. "I lay down my life for the sheep," John 10:15. "Therefore doth the Father love me, because I lay down my life, that I may take it again. No one taketh it away from me, but I lay it down of myself," John 10:17, 18.

It is not enough to recognize Christ as a teacher while rejecting Him as the atoning Saviour. In the conversation with Nicodemus He promptly brushed aside the complimentary words, "we know that thou art a teacher come from God," and declared that until one is born anew he cannot even so much as see the kingdom of God. And similarly the pity of the "Daughters of Jerusalem," although doubtless sincere, was rejected apparently because it did not recognize the fact that His suffering was not for Himself but for others, — "Weep not for me, but weep for yourselves," Luke 23:28. And the rending of the veil of the temple, which symbolized that the way into the presence of God had been opened for all men, occurred not at His baptism, nor at the Sermon on the Mount, but at His death.

The same teaching concerning the death of Christ is found throughout the New Testament. The Apostle Paul, for instance, pointedly conscious that he had received the cleansing which comes through faith in Christ, places His atoning death at the very heart of his theological system. "Christ redeemed us from the curse of the law, having become a curse for us," Gal. 3:13. "Him who knew no sin He [that is, God] made to be sin on our behalf [that is, laid on Him the punishment due for sin]; that we might become the righteousness of God in Him," 2 Cor. 5:21. "Christ died for our sins according to the Scriptures," 1 Cor. 15:3. He is the One whom "God set forth to be a propitiation, through faith, in His blood," Rom. 3:25. "I determined not to know anything among you, save Jesus Christ and Him crucified," 1 Cor. 2:2.

Peter declares that "Christ also suffered for sins once, the righteous for the unrighteous, that He might bring us to God," 1 Peter 3:18; and again that He "bare our sins in His body upon the tree," 1 Peter 2:24. John says, "The blood of Jesus His Son cleanseth us from all sin," 1 John 1:7; and "He is the propitiation for our sins," 1 John 2:2. "Apart from shedding of blood there is no remission," wrote the author of the Epistle to the Hebrews, 9:22; and again, "Now once at the end of the ages hath He been manifested to put away sin by the sacrifice of Himself," 9:26. And in John's Revelation the triumphant Christ is pictured as "arrayed in a garment sprinkled with blood," 19:13.

Even in the Old Testament this doctrine was clearly anticipated. In the Messianic 53rd chapter of Isaiah we read: "He was wounded for our transgressions, He was bruised for our iniquities; the chastisement of our peace was upon Him; and with His stripes we are healed. All we like sheep have gone astray; we have turned every one to his own way: and Jehovah hath laid on Him the iniquity of us all...He was cut off out of the land of the living for the transgression of my people to whom the stroke was due...When thou shalt make His soul an offering for sin...He shall justify many; and He shall bear their iniquities...He bare the sin of many, and made intercession for the transgressors," vss. 5-12.

In appointing the lamb as the principal animal for the morning and evening sacrifice in ancient Israel, God chose the animal which is at one and the same time the most harmless and gentle and the most attractive and pleasing of all the domestic animals, and thus emphasized both the innocence and the inherent value of the victim whose life was taken. The people were thus taught that their sins were forgiven and their lives spared only because another who was innocent and virtuous took their place and died in their stead. The term "Lamb of God," when applied to Christ, calls to mind the Old Testament sacrifices and invariably refers to His sacrificial death. John the Baptist, for instance, pointed out Jesus as "the Lamb of God, that taketh away the sin of the world," John 1:29. Peter says that we were redeemed, "not with corruptible things, with silver or gold...but with precious blood, as of a lamb without blemish and without spot, even the blood of Christ," 1 Peter 1:18, 19. In the Book of Revelation the redeemed are portrayed as those who have "washed their robes, and made them white in the blood of the Lamb," 7:14. And since Christ in His relationship with His people manifests so preeminently the attributes of gentleness and tenderness, and since He rules them in and through love, we are further given to understand that all opposition to Him is unprovoked and malignant.

Significance of the Term "Blood"

The term "blood" as used in theological language is, of course, to be understood as a figure of speech. It is used as a synonym for Christ's atoning death, and it designates the price which He paid for the redemption of His people. There are, as might be expected, many in our day who take offense at the term "blood," and wish to earn their salvation by their own good works. But the New Testament, as if anticipating this very offense, not only repeatedly asserts that salvation is not by works, but makes direct reference to the "blood" of Christ some thirty-five or forty times; and in the Old Testament there are innumerable references to the blood of the animals which were used in the ceremonies and rituals which prefigured the death of Christ. Salvation in all ages has been through Christ alone; and the Old Testament saints who worshipped God in His appointed way of sacrifice and poured-out blood looked to the same Saviour as do we who live in the Christian era. "The life of the flesh is in the blood," said the Lord to Moses, "and I have given it to you upon the altar to make atonement for your souls: for it is the blood that maketh atonement by reason of the life," Lev. 17:11. When the blood is poured out, the person or animal dies. Under the ceremonial law the blood with which atonement was made was secured in such a way that the life of the victim was always forfeited. In the twelfth chapter of Exodus we are given an account of the Passover, with its sprinkling of blood and the deliverance of all the firstborn of Israel from death. On the day of annual Atonement the high priest was to sprinkle the blood of the bullock and of the goat over the mercy seat and upon the horns of the altar, Lev. 16:1-34. The various Old Testament blood rituals were but prophetic types or prefigurements of the great sacrifice which later was to be made by Christ when He offered Himself for the sins of His people.

The teaching of the New Testament concerning the blood is very explicit. We have seen that Jesus' own words in instituting the Lord's Supper were, "This is my blood of the covenant, which is poured out for many unto remission of sins," Matt. 26:28. Paul repeatedly asserts this truth: "Now being justified by His blood, we shall be saved from the wrath of God through Him," Rom. 5:9. "Jesus Christ…in whom we have our redemption through His blood, the forgiveness of our trespasses, according to the riches of His grace," Eph. 1:3, 7. "But now in Christ Jesus ye that once were afar off are made nigh in the blood of Christ," Eph. 2:13. Christ has "made peace through the blood of His cross," Col. 1:20. The writer of the Epistle to the Hebrews, contrasting the work of Christ with that of the high priest in ancient Israel, says that "Christ having come a high priest…not through the blood of goats and calves, but through His own blood, entered in once for all into the holy place, having obtained eternal redemption. For if the blood of goats and bulls, and the ashes of a heifer sprinkling them that have been defiled, sanctify unto the cleanness of the flesh: how much more shall the blood of Christ, who through the eternal Spirit offered Himself without blemish unto God, cleanse your conscience from dead works to serve the living God?"

Heb. 9:11-14. John writes, "The blood of Jesus His Son cleanseth us from all sin," 1 John 1:7. And in the songs of praise to the Redeemer, recorded in the book of Revelation, we hear the words, "Worthy art thou to take the book, and to open the seals thereof: for thou wast slain, and didst purchase unto God with thy blood men of every tribe, and tongue, and people, and nation.... Worthy is the Lamb that hath been slain to receive the power, and riches, and wisdom, and might, and honor, and glory, and blessing," Rev. 5:9, 12.

So let no one take offense at the term "blood." Since salvation was purchased for us by the vicarious suffering and death of Christ, and since that suffering and death is symbolized by the blood, it is but natural that both the Old and the New Testament should mention the blood repeatedly. Many persons have tried to gain salvation by other methods, by church membership, pledge signing, good resolutions, meritorious works, etc., only to find that such methods invariably end in failure. So clearly and constantly and emphatically do the New Testament writers assert that the efficacy of Christ's work is to be ascribed to His death, His blood, His cross, that we are justified in asserting that the Scripturalness or un-Scripturalness of the various present day theories of the atonement can be fairly tested by the place which they give to His death.

To the unsaved nothing seems more unreasonable and meaningless than the assertion that salvation is to be obtained through the blood of Christ. The Scriptures, of course, recognize this condition of the unregenerate heart, and declare that, "The word of the cross is to them that perish foolishness," and then add by way of contrast, "but unto us who are saved it is the power of God," 1 Cor. 1:18. Those who have experienced the cleansing and forgiveness which comes through this faith know that the crucified and risen Lord is able to save to the uttermost those who draw near unto God through Him, and that there is no salvation in any other.

And unless Christ did thus give His life a sacrifice for others we are at a loss to know why He died. We have seen that the penalty which God originally prescribed for sin was the loss of life,—and like any other penalty it can be justly inflicted only where the law has been violated. But Christ suffered the penalty of death even though He had no sin of His own. Consequently He must have died for the sins of others. Unless He did thus die, His voluntary surrender to death, and that at the early age of thirty-three, must be looked upon as utter foolishness, as, in fact, criminal suicide.

Not Merely a Martyr's Death

There are many who deny that the death of Christ had any value as an atonement. The most common alternative view is that He died merely as a martyr. But apart from the fact that a mere martyr's death would leave most of the distinctive Christian doctrines without any adequate foundation, the narratives themselves make it quite clear that something profoundly different was involved. Compare His feeling, in view of death, with that of Paul: "having the desire to depart," Phil. 1:23; "The time of my departure is come. I have fought the good fight, I have finished the course, I have kept the faith: henceforth there is laid up for me the crown of righteousness, which the Lord, the righteous judge, shall give to me at that day; and not to me only, but also to all them that love His appearing," 2 Tim. 4:6-8. Jesus, on the other hand, was filled with anguish. "Now is my soul troubled; and what shall I say? Father, save me from this hour," John 12:27. We are told that "His sweat became as it were great drops of blood falling down upon the ground," Luke 22:44. And as He hung on the cross we hear the despairing cry, "My God, my God, why hast thou forsaken me?" Matt. 27:46. As Dr.

A. H. Strong has said, "If Christ was simply a martyr, then He was not a perfect example; for many a martyr has shown greater courage in prospect of death, and in the final agony has been able to say that the fire which consumed him was 'a bed of roses.' Gethsemane, with its mental anguish, is apparently recorded in order to indicate that Christ's sufferings even on the cross were not mainly physical sufferings."

As Jesus hung on the cross He was, in His human nature, the true sin-offering for His people, and as such, it was necessary that He suffer alone. God can have no association whatever with sin, since in His sight it is infinitely heinous. And, as in the Old Testament ritual for the sin-offering, this was symbolized by the burning of the flesh of the bullock outside of the camp (even the offering itself being treated as offensive and polluted since in the mind of the offerer it stood representative of and was in some way associated with his sin), so Jesus, as He bore in His own body the full weight of the penalty of sin, was temporarily cut off from the Father's presence and paid the entire cost of redemption without help from any other. The darkened heavens, and the cry, "My God, my God, Why hast thou forsaken me?" indicate as much. He was acutely conscious not only of the pain from the nails, but also of a break in that intimate and loving fellowship which He had always enjoyed with the Father. Since Jesus in His human nature was subject to the limitations which are common to men, it was as possible for Him to experience the sense of separation from the Father as it was for Him to be ignorant of the time of the end of the world, or to suffer pain or hunger. But during the crucifixion, as He bore a burden of sin such as had never been borne and could never be borne by any mere man, He went through an experience far more awful and terrifying than is possible for any mere martyr. In contrast with His sufferings, the Christian martyrs were deeply conscious of God's presence as they yielded up their lives. If Christ's death was only a martyr's death it might well fill us with terror and despair, for it would show that the holiest man who ever lived was utterly forsaken by God in the hour of His greatest need.

Death is primarily the separation of the soul from God; and physical death, or the separation of the soul from the body, is only a by-product and a relatively unimportant consequence of that greater catastrophe. Jesus did not suffer the pangs which are experienced by lost souls in hell, but in paying the penalty for His people, He did suffer death in its most essential nature, which is separation from God. And while His sufferings were not identical, either in intensity or in length of time endured, with those which His people would have suffered had they been left to their own sin, in view of the infinite worth and dignity of the Sufferer they were nevertheless a full equivalent for those sufferings.

Let us keep in mind that it was not Christ's divine nature, but only His human nature, which was subject to suffering and death, as it was only His human nature which was subject to temptation, hunger, thirst, sleep, etc. While we do not fully understand the relationship which exists between His two natures, we have a faint analogy in our own persons in which a spiritual and a physical nature are united; and on the basis of our own experience we know that what He experienced in either nature He experienced as a person, that is, as the God-man. This latter fact is of the utmost importance since it explains why His work of redemption was possessed of infinite value, sufficient to save all those who put their trust in Him. And again, while we do not fully understand the relationship which exists between the two natures, and while the analogy does not hold at all points, we may picture His divine nature during the crucifixion as not only fully sympathetic with His human nature, but as looking down upon His human nature calmly and serenely as the moon in its majesty looks down upon the troubled sea.

It seems quite evident that the work of redemption, which together with its wider effects may also be designated as the spiritual re-creation of the souls of men, was a greater work than the original creation of the universe. When the starry heavens were brought into existence and spread throughout the vast bounds of space, that work, while requiring great power and wisdom, was accomplished at God's spoken command. Such creation was comparatively easy, and is referred to as but "the work of His finger," Ps. 8:3. "He spake, and it was done; He commanded, and it stood fast," Ps. 33:9. But when the work of redemption was to be accomplished, God, in the person of Christ, took upon Himself human nature with its attendant weaknesses, was born a helpless babe in low condition, underwent the hardships of this life, was scoffed at and rejected by the religious and political rulers of the nation, suffered the cruel pain and cursed death of the cross, was buried, and continued under the power of death for a time. While the work of creation was accomplished through a mere exercise of power and wisdom, the work of redemption was accomplished only at an infinite cost of suffering on the part of God Himself. As man's soul is of incomparably greater value than his body, so the redemption of the souls of men was an incomparably greater work than the original creation of the universe. Christ's work of redemption is now seen to have been the central event of all history.

We do not mean to imply that man's salvation was completed by the work of Christ on the cross. His words, "I have accomplished the work which thou hast given me to do," John 17:4, and "It is finished," John 19:30, relate to the objective atonement which He provided for the sins of men. But the great purpose of His coming, that of making men subjectively just and holy, was not yet fulfilled. As the work of providence follows the work of creation, so the subjective cleansing of the sinner is a continuing process as the redemption which was purchased by Christ is applied by the Holy Spirit to those for whom it was intended. Here enter the works of regeneration, justification, adoption, sanctification, and glorification. But this opens up a whole new field of theology, that of the person and work of the Holy Spirit, which we have not space to discuss in this present work.

Thus the death of Christ emerges as the central truth in the Christian doctrine of redemption. It is the link which holds together all of the other distinctive doctrines. The mark of His blood is upon them all and signifies their ownership, as the scarlet thread running through every cord and rope of the British navy signifies that it is the property of the crown. It hardly seems possible that, with this central truth written so plainly and so repeatedly across the pages of Scripture, any honest or serious minded persons could arise, as do the Unitarians and Modernists, and declare that the essence of Christianity consists in our following the example of Christ in lives of social service, or that the chief purpose of the Church is to build a new social order in this world. It is very evident, of course, that in our daily lives we are to follow the example of Christ as closely as possible. And in due course of time a new social order, based on justice and improved living conditions, will gradually arise as Christian principles are applied first to the lives of individuals and through them to the life of the community. In many limited social groups we already see the effects of this uplifting process. But Christ's expiatory death is no more an object for our imitation than is the creation of the world. For in His death He took man's place and rendered to divine justice a satisfaction which man himself was utterly unable to render. That Christianity is not primarily a social movement, but a redemptive religion, setting forth a way of escape from sin, is as plain as it is possible for words to make it.

III. The Satisfaction View of the Atonement

Before we can have any adequate understanding or appreciation of the work that Christ has done for us it is necessary that we know something of the nature and effect of sin in the human soul. In substance the Bible tells us that sin is open and defiant rebellion against the law of God. There are, of course, many forms in which it may manifest itself, such as murder, robbery, adultery, lying, profanity, idolatry, pride, envy, covetousness, disrespect for parents, etc. But regardless of the different forms which it may assume it is essentially and definitely one thing: It is crime committed against God. Perhaps the best known formal definition of sin is that of the Westminster Confession which says, "Sin is my want of conformity unto, or transgression of, the law of God." The law of God is moral in the highest sense, and has been given for the good of mankind. It is a revelation of, or a transcript of, God's own character, and is therefore perfect and immutable.

The person who commits sin transfers his allegiance from God to the Devil, although but few seem to realize that they are actually serving the Devil. But the Scripture says, "He that doeth sin is of the Devil," 1 John 3:8. Paul was divinely appointed to preach to the Gentiles, "to open their eyes, that they may turn from darkness to light and from the power of Satan unto God," Acts 26:18. We have the word of Jesus that "Every one that committeth sin is the bond-servant of sin" John 8:34;

and to the Pharisees who maliciously opposed Him He said, "Ye are of your father the Devil, and the lusts of your father it is your will to do," John 8:44.

The nature of sin being what it is, it is not surprising that the penalty that God has established against it is severe. That penalty is *death*, "In the day that thou eatest thereof thou shalt surely die," Gen. 2:17, was the clearly announced penalty spoken to Adam at the very beginning of the race. It was repeated by the prophets, e.g., "The soul that sinneth, it shall die." Ezek. 18:4; and in the New Testament, "The wages of sin is death," Rom. 6:23.

We have already pointed out that death in this sense included a great deal more than physical death, which is the separation of the soul from the body, that it was primarily spiritual death, or the eternal separation of the soul from God. In this broader sense death means an abandoned spiritual condition such as that of the Devil and the demons. It involves the immediate loss of the divine favor, the sense of guilt, the corruption of the moral nature (resulting of course in the commission of other and more flagrant transgressions), and the pains of hell. The reward promised for obedience, as is clearly implied in the Genesis account and in later Scripture, was *life*, the exact opposite of the penalty threatened, not merely physical life as we know it, but eternal life such as is enjoyed by the holy angels. And since Adam by divine appointment stood representative for all of those who were to come after him by natural descent and acted precisely as they would have acted under similar circumstances, the reward for his obedience or the penalty for his disobedience was designed to fall not only on him but equally on them. Thus situated, Adam made his choice,—and fell. The results were disastrous, for by that fall he brought himself and his descendants into a state of depravity, guilt, and condemnation, a state in which the intellect is blinded to spiritual truth, the affections corrupted, and the will enslaved. From that condition there was no possible way of escape—except by divine grace.

That the penalty for sin did relate primarily to man's spiritual nature is seen in the fact that Adam did not die a physical death for 930 years after he had disobeyed, although he died spiritually and felt himself estranged from God the very instant he sinned. It is also shown by the fact that Adam's unregenerate posterity since that time have invariably and persistently gone the way of evil, displaying the same aversion to righteousness and the same affection for sin.

Unchangeable Nature of the Law Against Sin

The moral law which God gave to man in the beginning was no arbitrary or whimsical pronouncement, but an expression of His being. It showed man what the nature of God was, and was designed to bring man's nature into closer conformity with His nature. It was very explicit, both in its command and in its threatened penalty. Now sin is the absolute contradiction of that nature, and cannot therefore be lightly set aside. In all of His dealings God reveals Himself as a holy, just, and truthful God. As a holy God He hates sin and burns against it with a consuming zeal. As a just God he scrupulously rewards righteousness and punishes sin, for strict justice is as insistent in its demand that sin shall be punished as it is in its demand that righteousness shall be rewarded. God cannot give the reward of obedience for disobedience. The same God who is a God of mercy and who in virtue of His mercy desires to save human souls, is also a God of justice and in virtue of His justice must punish sinners. And as a truthful God He must put into effect the penalty which He has said would be enforced against transgressors. For Him to fail to punish sin would be for Him to remove the penalty against it, to consent to it or to become partaker in it, and therefore to violate His own nature and to destroy the moral order of the universe. Consequently when sin is committed it simply cannot be ignored or cancelled out with mere pardon. The penalty must be paid. God's honor and justice are at stake. However much God in His love might have desired to have saved man, it was not possible for Him to do so until satisfaction was made to the divine law. Hence the truth of the Scripture statement: "Apart from shedding of blood [i.e., the payment of the prescribed death penalty] there is no remission" (of sin), Heb. 9:22.

Hence even if man possessed the power to repent and turn to God, forgiveness could not be granted on the basis of mere repentance. For repentance does not expiate crime, even under civil government. The fact that the murderer, or robber, or adulterer, or liar is sorry does not excuse him from obligation. He must restore what he has taken. He must make right what he has made wrong. Otherwise the injury remains. We instinctively feel that wrong-doing must be balanced by a corresponding penalty. This feeling is especially noticeable after a particularly atrocious crime has been committed. We say that the crime calls for vengeance, and that a moral order which would allow it to go unpunished would not be right. The truly penitent man never feels that his repentance constitutes a ground of acceptance, either with God or with his fellow men. The more sincerely he repents the more truly he recognizes his need of reparation and expiation.

Fortunately for us, God meets the demands of His own holiness and justice and of man's conscience by Himself providing an atonement, a satisfaction. He does not forgive sin merely because He cares so little about it, nor because He is so exclusively the God of love that all other considerations fall into insignificance beside it; but in His own person and by the sacrifice of Himself He pays the penalty which frees man from obligation and provides that righteousness which alone admits him into heaven. For as Dr. Wm. C. Robinson has recently said, "The cross is not a compromise, but a substitution; not a cancellation, but a satisfaction; not a wiping off, but a wiping out in blood and agony and death." Thus mercy does not cheat justice. Holiness is rewarded, sin is punished, and the moral order of the universe is maintained in its perfection.

Years ago in England and in our own country there were debtor's prisons in which those who could not pay their debts were incarcerated. The law was inexorable. The man who had borrowed money and squandered or mismanaged it had to go to prison. He could not make things right merely by saying that he was sorry. Some one had to stand the loss, either the borrower or the person from whom it had been borrowed. But if a wealthy friend of the borrower came forward and paid the debt he was set free. In fact, in such a case his freedom became mandatory, for the law was satisfied. And so it is with the Christian doctrine of the atonement. Christ has done for His people exactly what a man does for his friend,—He has paid the debt for them. That is the meaning of the cross. God Himself assumed man's nature, and in that nature took man's place before His own law, suffered its penalty, and saved man through pure grace.

It must be perfectly evident to every one that if God allowed sin to go unpunished, or if He dealt with it in a free and loose manner, it would mean that justice had been cast to the winds and that He was governed by weak sentimentality. In the original creation God made man in His own image and implanted in him a deep sense of moral responsibility. He would be unfaithful to Himself if after having implanted that great principle He did not rule in accordance with it. For He is not only a loving Father, but also a righteous Judge. He cannot permit His righteous laws to be violated with impunity. If the sinner is to be forgiven, then for his own sake as well as for the sake of truth and righteousness, that forgiveness must not come in such a way as to diminish or benumb his sense of guilt. While God's love and tenderness are manifested in His forgiveness of sin, that forgiveness must not be accomplished in a manner which fails to show sin to be what it really is, something hateful and painful to God, diametrically opposed to His holy nature and subversive of His rule throughout the universe. Otherwise man will be misled into an easy-going, good-natured carelessness, and will have no adequate understanding or appreciation of the favor that has been granted to him.

For the righteousness of God is not, as so many people seem inclined to believe, mere disinterested benevolence which can pass lightly over sin. It is rather a distinct and separate attribute of the divine nature which demands that sin shall receive its adequate punishment. We regret that so much of our modern theological literature shows an almost complete lack of any adequate sense of the heinousness and guilt of sin. It is only when men hold superficial views of sin and think that it can be cast off by simple repentance that they deny the need of an expiatory atonement. But in proportion as an aroused conscience tells us that we are sinners we realize how deep is our guilt and cry out for that Saviour who alone is "able to save to the uttermost them that draw near unto God through Him."

Holiness is Prior to and Conditions Love

The most fundamental attribute of God's nature is, not love, but holiness. His holiness may be defined as His self-perpetuating righteousness or purity, in virtue of which He eternally wills and maintains His own moral excellence. He has constituted the universe, and humanity as a part of it, so that it shall express His holiness,—positively by connecting happiness with righteousness, and negatively by connecting unhappiness or suffering with sin. Love, in itself, is irrational and capricious except as it is governed by holiness. And the fact that holiness is logically prior to and conditions love makes it impossible for sin to be pardoned without an atonement. There must be an adequate infliction of misery to offset that sin. Many of the Greek gods were notoriously immoral. But our God is a God of holiness, a God of perfect morality; and He can tolerate no sin. If the forgiveness of sin depended only on the sovereign will of God, there would, of course, be no need for an atonement. In Mohammedanism, for instance, where the sovereignty of God is so emphasized that all other attributes are dwarfed beside it, no need is felt for satisfying divine justice. Mohammedanism holds that God can pardon whom He will, and on whatever grounds He pleases. The immeasurable superiority of Christian theology is evidenced by its clear and emphatic demand that the justice and holiness of God must be maintained and that the affront which has been offered to it by human sin shall not go unpunished. The tendency in some modern systems of theology is to merge holiness and love and to assume that God can forgive sin without an atonement. But such an easy-going optimism either does not know what the holiness of God involves, or fails utterly to understand the heinous nature of sin.

That God is love is, of course, one of the clear revelations of Scripture. And to us who would be forever lost if it were not for His love, that is the crowning revelation of Christianity. But love is not all that God is, and can therefore never adequately express all that God is. It is equally true that God is just and that He must punish sin. The writer of the Epistle to the Hebrews says that His attitude toward the workers of iniquity is that of "a consuming fire" (12:29). The popular literature of our day abounds with many ill-considered assertions of the indiscriminate love of God, as though He were too broadly good to hold man to any real account for sin. But we can never know the depth of the meaning of God's love until it is thrown up against the background of those other lofty conceptions which arise from and are based on a true view of His holiness, righteousness and justice. In brief, we may say that whereas the Modernist reasons, God is love and therefore there is no need for an atonement, the truth is, God is love and therefore He provides an atonement.

This brings us to the question, What is true love? We may say that one person truly loves another when he has a greater desire to please that person than he has to please himself. And the correlated truth is: One person truly loves another when he would rather suffer himself than see that one suffer. In the final analysis there are just two moral principles which may govern one's action: the first is that which has one's own interests as its final motive or supreme object, and is therefore the *selfish* principle; the second is that which has the interests of others as its final motive and is therefore the self-giving, *sacrificial* principle. This second is the principle which God manifests in His relations with His people. Consequently the greatest message that any one can hear is that "*God is love*," (1 John 4:16); for that means that God's holy nature seeks to express itself actively toward him, and that he will therefore be fitted for the divine presence.

On Calvary more than anywhere else the great loving heart of God has been revealed to man. There was love, unspeakable love, "When God the mighty Maker died for man the creature's sin." This redeeming love originated in the Trinity and was first exhibited in God's attitude toward man, not in man's attitude toward God; for man showed only opposition and hatred for everything that was good. "Herein is love, not that we loved God, but that He loved us, and sent His Son to be the propitiation for our sins," 1 John 4:10. "God commendeth His own love towards us, in that, while we were yet sinners, Christ died for us," Rom. 5:8. The atonement is not the cause, but the effect, of God's love for His people. Because He loved them He redeemed them. In the cross there was revealed to us the love of the Father who proposed the covenant of grace, the love of the Son who in His own body freely accomplished that redemption, and the love of the Holy Spirit who makes that love effective in our hearts. This general thought has been beautifully expressed in a recent book by Dr. Wm. C. Robinson. Says he: "In the very being of God Himself there are eternal love relationships. 'God is love.' And hence out of that self-moving and self-motivated love ever existing between the Persons of the adorable Trinity love came forth into this world of sin. Out of God's great eternal love, out of the heart of the Trinity came the love of Calvary. Before the foundation of the world He did in love predestinate us unto the adoption of sons through Jesus Christ unto Himself (Eph. 1:4, 5). The eternal Son brought the love of heaven into this world of hate, and lifted it so high on that hill called a skull that every nation shall behold its light, every age be mellowed by its glow,"[1]

The great classical passage with reference to the Atonement is Rom. 3:25, 26. There Christ is declared to be the One "Whom God set forth to be a propitiation, through faith, in His blood, to show His righteousness because of the passing over of the sins done aforetime, in the forebearance of God; for the showing, I say, of His righteousness at this present season: that He might Himself be just, and the justifier of him that hath faith in Jesus." Here we are told, (1) that God set forth Christ as an effective propitiatory offering; (2) that man is saved by the exercise of faith in the substitutionary suffering and death of Christ; (3) that while up to this time God, in His mercy and in anticipation of the certain coming

---

1 *The Word of the Cross*, p. 118.

of a Redeemer, had saved men without exacting an adequate punishment for their sins. He determines that at this time He will provide that adequate and public exhibition of the punishment of sin; and (4) that the purpose of this sacrifice is that God Himself may be just while forgiving and saving the sinner. Because God had in pre-Christian times saved sinners while allowing their sins to go unpunished His own righteousness had been lost sight of and obscured, and it was necessary that an adequate exhibition of the punishment of sin be made before men and angels. The sacrifices of animals in Old Testament times were not real atonements, but only signs and tokens pointing to the real atonement which was to come later. As the Baptist theologian, Dr. A. H. Strong, has boldly expressed it, "Before Christ's sacrifice, God's administration was a scandal,—it needed vindication. The Atonement is God's answer to the charge of freeing the guilty."

Hence the first and primary effect of the atonement is upon God Himself in that through it He is enabled to remain righteous even when pardoning the sinner,—"that He might Himself be just, and the justifier of him that hath faith in Jesus." Because God Himself, in the person of Christ, has borne the penalty for sin, He is now able to show Himself as perfectly just and holy while at the same time He grants forgiveness and eternal life to those who put their faith in Christ.

CHRIST ALONE ABLE TO REDEEM MEN

We have said that man's condition after the fall was one of absolute helplessness, that he was morally alienated from God, and that his whole attitude toward God, so far as he thought of God at all, was one of opposition and enmity. In Scripture language he was "dead" in trespasses and sins (Eph. 2:1, 5). In that fallen state, however, he was still able to do works which considered only in themselves or in reference to his fellow men were good,—he was still able to love his family, to deal honestly with his neighbors, to feed the hungry and comfort the sorrowing, etc. But in doing these things he acted only from selfish or humanitarian motives. In no instances were they done with the purpose of honoring or glorifying God. He might give a million dollars to build a hospital, but he could not give so much as a cup of cold water to a disciple *in the name of Christ*. However good his works might appear in themselves, none of them were done with right motives toward God. All of them, therefore, had a vitiating principle, a fatal defect, and could in no wise merit salvation. Man's vital need, then, was not good advice, nor an impressive example of right conduct, but to be "made alive" spiritually (Eph. 2:1, 5), to be "born anew" (John 3:3), to experience "regeneration" and "renewing" by the Holy Spirit (Titus 3:5).

Since men were in that ruined and helpless condition there was only one possible way by which they might be saved. That was for another person of infinite value and dignity to take upon himself their nature, that is, human nature, and, with the consent of God, suffer the penalty which was due to them. His higher personality would give unlimited value to his suffering, which would then be a just equivalent for that which was due to them. And at this point comes in the importance of the Christian doctrine of the Trinity. For God is not only unity, but tri-personality, so that there are within the Godhead three Persons, each possessing full Deity, the same in substance and equal in power and glory. Hence because of this fact alone it was possible that there might be One who would offer Himself as Mediator between God and man, One possessing a personality of infinite value and dignity who therefore as man's Agent could work out an atonement of infinite value. Christ, the second Person of the Trinity, did offer Himself as such a Mediator between God and man.

In order to accomplish that work He became incarnate, uniting Deity and humanity in His person as intimately and harmoniously as our souls and bodies are united in ours. Only Christ, then, in His Divine-human person, that is, as the God-man, was qualified to accept that penalty and discharge that obligation. No other person in all the universe was capable of assuming that role. The sacrifice of no creature could have availed anything. Nor could either the Father or the Holy Spirit as such have performed that work. Only the two-natured Christ was capable of providing redemption. And only in His organic and official union with His people can we find that vital relation which makes His vicarious suffering either possible or just. The entire Bible from Genesis to Revelation is God's account of the work that He has done for man. In strict literalness it might have been called, "The History of Redemption," for the main features dealt with are the original creation of man, his fall, his condition after the fall, God's merciful staying of the full execution of the penalty, the long course of preparation for the coming of the Redeemer, the nature of the work performed by the Redeemer when He did come, His ascension to heaven and His future coming when He shall assign all men their eternal rewards.

Consequently, we find that in the accomplishment of that work Christ did not die a natural death. The kind of death that He died was particularly designed to show that satisfaction was being made to divine justice, that somehow He was dying because the penalty of sin is death. Had He been unexpectedly assassinated, or died as a result of accident, or disease, or old age, there would have been no appearance of a satisfaction having been made to satisfy the demands of divine justice. But when He is placed as a criminal before a tribunal, accused, overpowered by the testimony of witnesses, officially condemned to death, and crucified and His life taken from Him in the very prime of His manhood, we are given to understand that on this righteous Person was inflicted the punishment due to criminals, to malefactors,—in short, the punishment due to us as sinners. He died not merely a corporal death, but a particular kind of death in which He experienced the severity of the divine vengeance against sin. By paralleling even in detail the Old Testament ritual for the sin-offering it was made plain that He was our sin-bearer. What He did and suffered He did and suffered, not for any sin of His own, but for that of His people, in their name and on their account. Hence Paul could say, and we can say with him, "I have been crucified with Christ; and it is no longer I that live, but Christ liveth in me." Gal. 2:20.

Since man's sin was directed against God, who is an infinitely holy and just Being, and since fallen man if left to himself would have continued to sin throughout endless ages as do the Devil and the fallen angels, it is very evident that nothing less than an atonement of infinite value could have rescued him from that condition. This does not mean that Christ suffered as much during the space of one lifetime as His people would have suffered in an eternity of punishment. But it does mean that since the divine and human natures were united in the person of Christ, His suffering possessed a value equal to or rather greater than that which all of His people deserved, and that it was therefore amply sufficient for the redemption of all who put their trust in Him. His suffering was not the same as theirs either in kind or in duration; for He could suffer no remorse because He had no personal sin, and His was terminated within a few hours whereas theirs, due to their endless persistence in sin, would have continued through all eternity. A finite being could never have exhausted that penalty, but an infinite Being can exhaust it in a comparatively short time. But while not identical with the sufferings that sinners would have borne, His sufferings were of such kind and degree and duration as divine wisdom, interpreting divine justice, decreed was a full legal equivalent of that penalty when suffered vicariously by a divine person. Only when Calvary is regarded as revealing eternal principles of the divine nature can we see how the sufferings of those few hours can suffice to save millions of mankind. Certainly the fundamental conception of Christ's redeeming work as it is set forth in the Scriptures is that through His vicarious suffering and death He made full satisfaction to the justice of God and by His vicarious obedience He has merited eternal life so that all those who by faith accept Him as their Lord and Savior receive, firstly, deliverance from the guilt of sin, so that they are no longer under obligation to suffer for it; secondly, emancipation from the power of sin, so that they are cleansed from it and enabled to live a holy life; and, thirdly, a life of eternal blessedness in heaven.

To those who are accustomed to look upon man as sufficient for all things, the death of Christ and redemption through blood atonement is, of course, nonsense. When it was first announced it was "unto Jews a stumblingblock, and unto Gentiles foolishness," but unto them that believed it was "the power of God, and the wisdom of God," 1 Cor 1:23. Some call it repulsive. It is indeed repulsive and humiliating to the self-confident natural man. When Unitarians and Modernists represent it as a cruel demand on God's part and as an expiation from without in which one man's sin is laid on another while they themselves profess to believe in a God of love, they consciously or unconsciously caricature the Christian doctrine. For the plain and repeated teaching of Scripture is that it was not an outsider but God Himself in the person of Christ who met the demands of His own justice in order that He might be free to save man. For "God was in Christ reconciling the world unto Himself," 2 Cor. 5:19. Nor is this doctrine difficult to understand. A little child can understand its essential features, and can receive it to the salvation of his soul. And certainly it is not a system of human invention, for all men naturally feel that they should earn salvation by their own good works. A system of salvation by grace is so radically at variance with what man sees in the natural world where every thing and person is evaluated in terms of works and merits that he has great difficulty in bringing Himself to believe that it can be true. There is real point in the words of the great English preacher, C. H. Spurgeon: "The doctrine of substitution must be true; it could not have been invented by human wit." In one way or another all of the pagan religions and all of the philosophical systems teach that man must earn his own salvation. Christianity alone sets forth a system of salvation by grace. Time and again the Scriptures repeat the assertion that salvation is by grace, as if anticipating the difficulty which men would have in coming to the conclusion that they could not earn it by their own good works.

The Difference Between Commercial and Penal Debt

It has sometimes been charged that the satisfaction view represents the sacrifice of Christ as a purely commercial transaction. There is, however, a wide difference. In a commercial or pecuniary debt the point is not *who pays*, but *what is paid*, and the payment of the thing owed *ipso facto* frees the debtor from any further obligation whatsoever. If a third person offers to pay the debt, the creditor has no other choice than to accept the payment. He then has no further claim on the person of the debtor. He cannot be said to have extended any grace or indulgence toward the debtor; for he has received the precise *thing* which was due him. But penal debt is far different. In this case the obligation rests upon the *person* as well as upon the thing due. Not only must the prescribed penalty be suffered, but it must be suffered by the person who has committed the crime. A vicarious suffering of the penalty is permissible only at the discretion of the sovereign or judge. If it is permitted, it is a matter of grace to the criminal; and the rights which are acquired by the vicarious suffering all accrue to the sponsor or substitute who has borne the suffering. The claims of the law upon the sinner are not automatically dissolved by such a transaction. Instead, the benefits are passed on to him only at such times and on such conditions as have previously been agreed upon between the sovereign and the sponsor. Hence it is that the benefits of Christ's suffering were not immediately set to the account of His people at the time He suffered, but accrue to them as individuals down through the ages, in greater or lesser degree, and in many varied conditions, in accordance with the terms of the secret covenant which was made between the Father, the Son and the Holy Spirit. Hence, too, it is that God is absolutely sovereign in bestowing these benefits, and that salvation is of pure grace. God can give or withhold these benefits in each individual case as He pleases. The vicarious suffering of Christ thus emerges as an infinite benefit to those who are saved, and as no injury or disadvantage whatever to any who may be left to bear the penal consequences of their own sin.

In the following illustration Dr. Robert L. Dabney, the noted theologian of the Southern Presbyterian Church, has brought out quite clearly the distinction between (1) commercial debt; (2) the satisfaction view; and (3) a compromise system in which something less than the equivalent of the original obligation is paid: "A mechanic is justly indebted to a land-owner in the sum of one hundred pounds; and has no money wherewith to pay. Now, should a rich brother offer the landlord the full hundred pounds, in coin of the realm, this would be a legal tender; it would, *ipso facto*, cancel the debt, even though the creditor captiously rejected it. Christ's satisfaction is not *ipso facto* in this commercial sense. There is a second supposition: that the kind brother is not rich, but is himself an able mechanic; and seeing that the landlord is engaged in building, he proposes that he will work as a builder for him two hundred days, at ten shillings *per diem* (which is a fair price), to cancel his poor brother's debt. This proposal, on the one hand, is not a 'legal tender,' and does not compel the creditor. He may say that he has already enough mechanics, who are paid in advance; so that he cannot take the proposal. But, if he judges it convenient to accept it, although he does not get the coin, he gets an actual equivalent for his claim, and a fair one. This is *satisfactio*. The debtor may thus get a valid release on the terms freely covenanted between the surety and the creditor" (—the same principle applying here as in the Reformed or Calvinistic system, which holds that Christ made a full satisfaction for the sins of His people). "But there is a third plan: The kind brother has some 'script' of the capital stock of some company, which, 'by its face' amounts nominally to one hundred pounds, but all know that it is worth but little. Yet he goes to the creditor, saying: 'My brother and I have a pride about bearing the name of full payment of our debt. We propose that you take this 'script' as one hundred pounds (which is its nominal amount), and give us a discharge, which shall state that you have payment in full.' Now, if the creditor assents, this is payment *per acceptilationem*" (the same principle applying here as in the Arminian system, which holds that since the sinner could not pay his debt God, as a result of Christ's suffering on the cross, no longer demands perfect obedience, but now offers salvation on lower terms, on the basis of such "faith and evangelical obedience" as the crippled sinner is able to offer). "Does Christ's satisfaction amount to no more than this? We answer emphatically, it does amount to more. This disparaging conception is refuted by many Scriptures, such as Is. 42:21; 50:6. It is dishonorable to God, representing Him as conniving at a 'legal fiction,' and surrendering all standards of truth and justice to confusion. On this scheme, it is impossible to see how any real necessity for satisfaction could exist. The Reformed assert then, that Christ made penal satisfaction, by suffering the very penalty demanded by the law of sinners." *Theology*, p. 504.

CONTRAST BETWEEN THE GOSPELS AND THE EPISTLES

In recent years some critics have attempted to discredit the doctrine of the atonement by setting the teaching of Jesus over against that of Paul. It is true, of course, that Jesus did not say a great deal about the atonement. A careful examination of His teaching, however, will show that its reality was constantly assumed, and that on some occasions He expressed it clearly. This lack of emphasis concerning it in the Gospels as compared with its repeated statement in the Epistles has led some to say that true Christianity is based on the former and that the latter must be rejected.

But the reason for this difference of approach is very evident when we remember that the primary purpose of Jesus in His earthly mission was not to preach the Gospel but to work out an atonement so that there might be a Gospel to preach, — to be the sacrifice rather than to speak of it. The cross had to be endured before it could be explained; and when we consider the slowness, or even the inability, of the apostles to grasp the meaning of the atonement until after the day of Pentecost this becomes all the more evident. Jesus Himself proclaimed the incompleteness of His own words, declaring that He had yet many things to say unto the apostles although they were not then able to bear them, and promising that the Holy Spirit who was soon to be given would guide them into all truth (John 16:12, 13). Furthermore, this reticence on the part of Jesus is just what we might have expected since the doer of a great deed usually has the least to say about it. It was not for the Redeemer, but for the redeemed, to magnify the cost of salvation.

Also in this connection we are to remember that in reality the Gospels are supplementary to the Epistles, not the Epistles to the Gospels as so many people are accustomed to assume,—the Epistles being more concerned with setting forth the great fact of redemption while the Gospels are mainly concerned with filling out our knowledge of the person of Christ and showing at what an infinite cost redemption was procured. The fact that the material in the Gospels deals almost exclusively with the events which occurred during the last three years of Jesus' life and that the closing scenes are given special prominence—approximately one-third of all the material being devoted to the events of the last week—is evidence that not His life, but His death, was the great work of our Lord. Furthermore, one of the two ordinances which He established, the Lord's Supper, was designed to keep His death prominently in the minds of His people. The fact is that the Gospels and the Epistles unite in affirming that the death of Christ lays the basis for our salvation.

The world at large has long been inclined to blame the Jews for the death of Christ, and the Jews in turn have been inclined either to deny it outright or to shift the blame to the Romans. But a truer analysis of the whole affair was recently given by a Jewish speaker addressing an American Jewish audience. After asking, "Did the Jews kill Christ?" he gave the answer in these words: "In a larger sense the death of Jesus was not an accident; the greed of the mercenary priests and the vacillation of Pontius Pilate the Roman, were merely incidental to it. The New Testament teaches that the death of Christ was a divine act, that His death was sacrificial; and the intelligent follower of Jesus, be he Jew or Gentile, does not shift the blame to the shoulders of

Jews, but assumes equal responsibility for the tragedy that took place on Golgotha's hill. There is a Christian litany which runs:

> *"Who was the guilty? Who brought this upon Thee?*
> *Alas my treason, Jesus, hath undone Thee.*
> *'Twas I, Lord Jesus, I it was denied Thee:*
> *I crucified Thee."*

"The cleavage of the centuries can be bridged. The misunderstandings and the hates which have kept Jew and Gentile apart can be removed by a common acknowledgment that in the person of the High Priest our people were led into a fatal act, and through Pontius Pilate and the Roman soldiery the whole Gentile world became sharers in the immolation of Christ. We are both guilty, Jew and Gentile, and have need to smite our breast and cry for the forgiveness of God."

A true understanding of the nature of the atonement makes it crystal clear that the responsibility for the death of Christ does rest on Jew and Gentile alike, and that it rests primarily upon all of us who were to be redeemed through the ages, and, heinous and cruel though it was, only secondarily and incidentally on the men of that generation who actually laid the burden of suffering upon Him.

IV. THE ACTIVE AND PASSIVE OBEDIENCE OF CHRIST

We have said that the two great objectives to be accomplished by Christ in His mission to this world were, first, the removal of the curse under which His people labored as a result of the fall, and, second, their restoration to the image and fellowship of God. It is perfectly evident that both of these elements were essential to salvation. In the preceding section we pointed out that because of the federal relationship which, through appointment of God, Adam bore to his posterity, all mankind since that time have been born into the state into which he fell, and that the purpose of Christ was to rescue His people from that condition and to bring them into a state of holiness and blessedness. In order that He might accomplish that purpose He entered into a vital relationship with them by taking their nature upon Himself through incarnation. Then, acting as their federal head and representative in precisely the same manner that Adam had acted when he plunged the race into sin, He assumed their place before the divine law, fulfilling, on the one hand, its every precept, and on the other, receiving in His own person the penalty due for their transgressions. He thus lived the particular kind of life and suffered the particular kind of death that we read of in the Gospels. These two phases of His work are known as His "Active" and His "Passive" obedience.

IV. The Active and Passive Obedience of Christ

Throughout the history of the Church most theological discussions have stressed Christ's passive obedience (although not often calling it by that name), but have had very little to say about His active obedience. The result is that many professing Christians who readily acknowledge that Christ suffered and died for them seem altogether unaware of the fact that the holy, sinless life which He lived was also a vicarious work in their behalf, wrought out by Him in His representative capacity and securing for them title to eternal life.

A moment's reflection should convince us that the suffering and death of Christ, although fully effective in paying the debt which His people owed to divine justice, was in a sense only a negative service. Being of the nature of a penalty it could relieve His people from the liability under which they labored, but it could not provide them with a positive reward. Its effect was to bring them back up to the zero point, back to the position in which Adam stood before the fall. It provided for their rescue from sin and its consequences, but it did not provide for their establishment in heaven. Life in heaven is the reward for the perfect keeping of the moral law through a probationary period. Had the work of Christ stopped with the mere payment of the debt which was owed by His people, then they, like Adam, would still have been under obligation to have earned their own salvation through a covenant of works and, also like Adam, subject again to eternal death if they disobeyed. But the covenant of works had had its day and had failed. Very evidently if salvation is to be attempted a second time it will be on a different plan. For what would be the sense of rescuing a man from a torrent which had proved too strong for him merely to put him back into the same situation? Having rescued His people once God would not permit them to be lost a second time and in precisely the same way. This time not man but God will be the Actor; not works but grace (which is the free and undeserved love or favor of God exercised toward the undeserving, toward sinners) will be the basis; and not failure but complete success will crown the effort. Hence Christ, in His human nature and as a perfectly normal man among men, rendered perfect obedience to the moral law by living a sinless life during the thirty-three years of His earthly career, and thus fulfilled the second and vitally important part of His work of redemption.

THE SINLESS LIFE OF CHRIST

That Christ did live this life of perfect love and unselfish service to God and man is clearly set forth in Scripture. He "did no sin, neither was guile found in His mouth," 1 Peter 2:22. He was "holy, guileless, undefiled, separated from sinners," says the writer of the Epistle to the Hebrews. 7:26. "I do always the things that are pleasing to Him," said Jesus, John 8:29. "Which of you convicteth me of sin?" was His challenge to His enemies, John 8:46. Even the demons bore witness that He was "the Holy One of God," Luke 4:34. As He was being crucified He prayed, "Father, forgive them." But never did He pray, Father, forgive me. It is not uncommon for the greatest of saints, when they come to the hour of death, to pour out their souls in fresh confessions; desiring to obtain renewed consciousness of sins forgiven. But there is no trace of sin-consciousness to be found anywhere in the life of Jesus. He made no confession of sin, nor did He at any time offer a sacrifice for Himself in the temple. At the time of His death there was no shadow of a cloud between Him and the Father except as He assumed the consequences of sin on behalf of others.

By that life of spotless perfection, then, Jesus acquired for His people a positive righteousness which is imputed to them and which secures for them life in heaven. All that Christ has done and suffered is regarded as having been done and suffered by them. In Him they have fulfilled the law of perfect obedience, as also in Him they have borne the penalty for their sins. By His passive obedience they have been rescued from hell; and by His active obedience they are given entrance into heaven.

SALVATION BY GRACE

Paul's teaching that we are saved, not by a self-acquired, but by an imputed righteousness is very clear and definite. He strongly rebuked those of His own race who, "being ignorant of God's righteousness, and seeking to establish their own, did not subject themselves to the righteousness of God," Rom. 10:3; and he declared that he willingly suffered the loss of all things in order that he might "gain Christ, and be found in Him, not having a righteousness of mine own, even that which is of the law, but that which is through faith in Christ," Phil. 3:9. "Him who knew no sin He made to be sin on our behalf; that we might become the righteousness of God in Him," 2 Cor. 5:21,—that is, our guilt and punishment was transferred to Christ, in order that His righteousness and purity might be transferred to us. To the Ephesians he wrote, "We are His workmanship, created in Christ Jesus for good works, which God afore prepared that we should walk in them," 2:10. Notice that he does not say that this change in character came about because we did good works, but that he ascribes the workmanship to God and says that its purpose was that we might bear fruit in good works and that these were not original on our part but that they were afore prepared or planned out that we should do them. In his declarations that, "If there had been a law given which could make alive, verily righteousness would have been of the law," Gal. 3:21, and "If righteousness is through the law, then Christ died for nought," Gal. 2:21, he disposes completely of the notion that man can earn his own salvation by good works. If we had been able to have worked out our own salvation there would have been no need for Christ to have become incarnate and to have submitted to such humiliation and suffering. And, of course, in that case He most certainly would not have done so. How profoundly grateful we should be that not only our suffering for sin, but also our probation for heaven, has been assumed for us by Christ, that each of these is now a thing of the past, and that we are safe forever in God's care!

The salvation which the Scriptures offer to mankind is therefore a salvation provided entirely by God Himself. It is not adulterated in any way by human works. And because it is of this nature the Scripture writers never tire of asserting that it is by grace and not by works. Even the faith through which salvation is received is induced by the Holy Spirit and is a gift: "By grace have ye been saved through faith; and that not of yourselves, it is the gift of God; not of works, that no man should glory," Eph. 2:8, 9. We are "justified freely by His grace," Rom. 3:24. Man's own righteousness, in the words of Isaiah, is as but "a polluted garment" (or, as the King James Version expresses it, "as filthy rags") in the sight of God, 64:6. "Not by works done in righteousness, which we did ourselves, but according to His mercy He saved us, through the washing of regeneration and renewing of the Holy Spirit," Titus 3:5. To Paul's assertion that Christ is "all, and in all" in matters of salvation, Col. 3:11, we can add that man is nothing at all as to that work, and has not anything in himself which merits salvation. We are, in fact, nothing but receivers; we never bring any adequate reward to God, and we are always receiving from Him, and shall be unto all eternity. Good works are in no sense the meritorious ground, but rather the fruits and proof of salvation. They are performed not with the purpose of earning salvation, but as an expression of love and gratitude for the salvation which has already been conferred upon us. Good works, done with right motives toward God, are a result of our having been regenerated, not the means of our regeneration. Our part in this system is to praise God, to honor Him by keeping His commandments, and to reflect His glory in all possible ways. And just because salvation is by grace and does not have to be earned by works it is possible even for one who repents on his death bed, or for one like the thief on the cross, to turn to Jesus in the last hour and be saved.

In another connection the present writer has said: "We hold that the law of perfect obedience which was originally given to Adam was permanent, that God has never done anything which would convey the impression that the law was too rigid in its requirements, or too severe in its penalty, or that it stood in need either of abrogation or of derogation. We believe that the requirement for salvation now as originally is perfect obedience, perfect conformity to the will and character of God, that the merits of Christ's obedience are imputed to His people as the only basis of their salvation, and that they enter heaven clothed only with the cloak of His perfect righteousness and utterly destitute of any merit properly their own. Thus grace, *pure grace*, is extended not in lowering the requirements for salvation, but in the substitution of Christ for His people. He took their place before the law and did for them what they could not do for themselves. This Calvinistic principle is fitted in every way to impress upon us the absolute perfection and unchangeable obligation of the law which was originally given to Adam. It is not relaxed or set aside, but fittingly honored so that its excellence is shown. In behalf of those who are saved, for whom Christ died, and in behalf of those who are subjected to everlasting punishment, the law in its majesty is enforced and executed."[2]

---

2 *The Reformed Doctrine of Predestination*, p. 154.

This doctrine of the sufficiency of Christ's work in regard both to His active and passive obedience is beautifully set forth in the Westminster Confession, which declares that "The Lord Jesus, by His perfect obedience and sacrifice of Himself, which He through the eternal Spirit offered up unto God, hath fully satisfied the justice of His Father; hath purchased not only reconciliation, but an everlasting inheritance in the kingdom of heaven, for all those whom the Father had given Him" (Ch. VIII, Sec. 5). And in the Shorter Catechism in answer to the question, "What is justification?" we are told that "Justification is an act of God's free grace, wherein He pardoneth all our sins, and accepteth us as righteous in His sight, only for the righteousness of Christ imputed to us, and received by faith alone."

But while it enables us to understand more clearly and fully the work which Christ has accomplished for us, if we view it as having an active and a passive side, we must not imagine that these two phases can be separated in His life. We cannot even say that His active obedience was accomplished by His life and His passive obedience by His death. For in varying degrees these two works were accomplished simultaneously and concurrently. Throughout all of His life He was perfectly obedient to the moral law in all that He thought and said and did. And in varying degrees every moment of His life on earth involved humiliation or suffering or both,—it involved humiliation beyond our power to comprehend for the King of Glory, the Creator of the universe, the One who is altogether holy and blessed and powerful and rich, to be born a helpless babe, and that in the most humble condition, to subject Himself to the limitations of incarnate man for a period of thirty-three years, to endure the temptations presented by the Devil, to bring His holy and sensitive nature into close association with sinful men so that He would hear their railings and curses and be confronted with their ingratitude and opposition and hatred, to experience fatigue and hunger, and to look forward through all of His public ministry to the most shameful and painful death by crucifixion. And nowhere else was His active obedience so prominently displayed as on the cross, for there in particular as He suffered He also resisted all temptation to doubt God, or hate His enemies, or commit the slightest offense against those who treated Him so shamefully. Throughout His entire life as He actively obeyed He passively endured, and as He passively endured He actively obeyed. These two aspects of His work, while distinct in nature, were inextricably intertwined in time. Together they secure the wonderful, full salvation which was wrought out vicariously for us.

THE CRUCIFIXION ON CALVARY

Death by crucifixion is, of course, horrible in the extreme. The usual procedure was that the crosspieces would be laid flat on the ground, the person then stretched upon it, and a soldier would drive iron spikes through the hands and feet into the rough wood. Then the cross with its attached victim would be lifted and set in the hole prepared for it. The person was left to writhe in his agony, with the swelling wounds, the parched thirst, the burning fever, until death brought the welcome release. Human ingenuity has never devised greater agony than crucifixion. Yet that is what Christ endured for us.

But not for a minute would we be understood as inferring that we can really fathom the depths of Christ's suffering. We are only given partial information concerning it. His physical suffering was that of a perfectly normal man in crucifixion. Yet that was not all, nor even the most important part, of His suffering. His cry, "My God, my God, why hast thou forsaken me?" indicates a spiritual suffering more intense and more baffling than the physical. We have already seen that the penalty originally inflicted for sin was not merely the separation of the soul from the body, which is physical death, but the separation of the soul from God, which is spiritual death. That Jesus suffered this latter form of the penalty as well as the former is attested by His despairing cry. During those hours that Jesus hung on the cross as the sin-offering for His people that unique spiritual relationship which had existed between His human soul and the Father, and which had so enriched Him during the entire period of His earthly life, was completely withdrawn. No glimpse of Divinity any longer broke in upon Him. God had literally hid His face from Him. His human soul, which in Gethsemane "began to be greatly amazed and sore troubled," was now entirely cut off from all divine enlightenment. Being limited in knowledge and comprehension as all human souls are, utterly distressed by the ordeal through which He was passing, and engaged in this last desperate combat with the Devil and the forces of the evil world which through His entire earthly career had sought untiringly to cause His downfall and to defeat His purpose, His human soul was unable to understand fully this complete abandonment of the righteous soul by God the Father.

Not only was all special grace withdrawn from Him, but also all common grace. No sedative was allowed to dull His pain. Ordinarily those who were sentenced to be crucified were given a stupefying drug, in order that their suffering might be somewhat alleviated. Doubtless the two thieves who were crucified at the same time received that treatment. But Jesus, realizing that such a drug would incapacitate Him for carrying the very burden of suffering for which He had come to that hour and that it would therefore defeat His purpose of redemption, rejected the wine and myrrh and determined to suffer with His senses fully alert. All of

His friends forsook Him. Only His enemies remained to taunt. His clothes (also a gift of common grace, clothes being designed since the time of the fall to cover the body and to serve as a restraint on human sin) were removed, leaving Him shamefully exposed to the vulgar rabble. The light, which is one of the greatest gifts of common grace, was denied Him, and for three hours He was left to suffer in the terrifying darkness. Calvary presents a spectacle such as had never been seen before and can never be seen again. For Jesus did not suffer and die passively, as one helplessly submitting to the inevitable, but actively, as one keeping a schedule or as one fulfilling a purpose. Had we been able to have looked within the soul of Christ we would have witnessed the most colossal struggle that the universe has ever known. Far from being the passive sufferer that He appeared to those who witnessed the crucifixion, He was upholding the pillars of the moral universe by rendering full satisfaction to divine justice. For as the sinner's substitute and in his stead Jesus stood before the awful tribunal of God,—before the Judge who abhors sin and burns against it with inexpressible indignation. Justice severe and inexorable was meted out. As He endured the break in the spiritual relationship with the Father He literally descended into hell; for hell is primarily separation from God, a condition the exact opposite of the blessed environment of the divine presence. This does not mean that His soul suffered remorse or any sense of guilt, which is one of the torments of lost souls; for He had no personal sin. Nor does it mean that this condition continued after His death. All was completed on the cross. When the allotted suffering was finished the divine light again broke in upon His soul, and we hear His triumphant cry, "It is finished" (that is, the atonement, God's objective provision for man's salvation, was completed); and that was followed almost immediately by the affectionate words, "Father, into thy hands I commend my spirit." Every detail of the account is so presented that we are compelled to recognize the full price of our redemption was paid for by Christ alone, without human assistance of any kind. And thus through the infinite mercy of God and in a manner that shall forever bring glory to His name there was made available a way, the only possible way, through which sinners might be saved.

And after all, does not this Christian doctrine of the atonement stand forth as the only reasonable and logical explanation of the suffering and death of Christ? God has so ordered this world that sin and suffering are inseparably connected. Where there is no sin God cannot under any conditions inflict suffering, — for the simple reason that it would be unjust for Him to punish an innocent person. Christ's suffering can have no other explanation than that it was vicarious, rendered not for Himself but for others. For there One who was sinless and undefined suffered the extreme of pain and agony and disgrace as though He were the worst of sinners. Unless Christ was acting on behalf of others and as their substitute, God Himself is put under eternal indictment for inflicting such suffering without a cause.

Moreover, if it be denied that Christ's suffering was vicarious and substitutionary, His voluntary acceptance of crucifixion is utterly unreasonable, — in fact it is scandalous, because suicidal. The plain teaching of Scripture is that He accepted this ordeal voluntarily. "I lay down my life for the sheep…No one taketh it from me, but I lay it down of myself," John 10:15, 18. Rebuking Peter for His well-intended but misguided use of the sword He said, "Put up the sword into the sheath: the cup which the Father hath given me, shall I not drink it?" John 18:11. Now it is perfectly evident, of course, that no creature, not even a sinless angel, has the right to dispose of his own life. That prerogative belongs only to the Creator to whom he belongs. But

Christ did have that right, because He was the King of the universe. Since He had within Himself divine as well as human life He could dispose of Himself without fatal or permanent injury either to Himself or to any other person. When seen in the light of the doctrines of *substitution, satisfaction, sacrifice*, the death of Christ appears as a great divine achievement, a glorious and unapproachable priestly action through which the suffering Messiah offered Himself in order that divine justice might be safeguarded and that sinful man might be reconciled to God. Logic drives us to the conclusion that the death of Christ on the cross was no ordinary death, but a mighty transaction through which God provided redemption for His people.

Unless Christ was what He claimed to be, Deity incarnate giving His life a ransom for many, the Unitarians and Modernists are right in saying that the doctrine of the Atonement is a colossal hoax and that it is ridiculous for anyone to believe that he can obtain salvation through faith in a mere man, a Jew, who was crucified in Palestine nineteen hundred years ago. Either the Christian system is true and we are saved through the supernatural work of Christ as the Bible teaches and as devout people in all ages have believed, or we are left to save ourselves through some humanistic or naturalistic system as skeptics and unbelievers have held.

On the basis of any teaching rightfully calling itself Christian the active and passive obedience of Christ emerges as the only basis of our spiritual and eternal life. Since the demand that sin must be punished was met by Him in His representative capacity, justice was not injured; and since His life of perfect obedience to the moral law was also rendered in His representative capacity, the gift of spiritual cleansing and of eternal life is now conferred upon His people as their right and privilege. He saves them from hell, and establishes them in heaven. There is no blessing in this world or in the next for which they should not give Christ thanks.

V. Christ As Our Ransomer

In numerous places in Scripture Christ's work of redemption is declared to have been accomplished through the payment of a *ransom*. Nowhere is this set forth more clearly than in our Lord's own teaching. "The Son of man came not to be ministered unto, but to minister, and to give His life a ransom for many," said He concerning His own mission, Matt. 20:28. These same words are repeated in Mark 10:45. Paul doubtless had these words in mind when he declared that Christ "gave Himself a ransom for all," 1 Tim. 2:6. To the Corinthians he wrote, "Ye are not your own; for ye were bought with a price," 1 Cor. 6:19, 20. The elders from the church at Ephesus were admonished to "feed the church of the Lord which He purchased with His own blood." Acts 20:28. "Christ redeemed us from the curse of the law, having become a curse for us," he wrote to the Galatians, 3:13. In the epistle to Titus he declares that Christ "gave Himself for us, that He might redeem us from all iniquity, and purify unto Himself a people for His own possession, zealous for good works," 2:14. While it is the privilege of a disciple to "lose" his life in the service of his Lord (Matt. 10:39; Luke 9:24), it was the part of the Lord to "give" His life voluntarily for His people (John 10:15; Gal. 2:20).

Closely parallel with this is Peter's teaching: "Ye were redeemed, not with corruptible things, with silver or gold, from your vain manner of life handed down from the fathers; but with precious blood, as of a lamb without blemish and without spot, even the blood of Christ," 1 Peter 1:18, 19. In his second epistle he warns against those who "bring in destructive heresies, denying even the Master that bought them," 2:1. And in the book of Revelation praise is ascribed to Christ in the words, "Thou wast slain, and didst purchase unto God with thy blood men of every tribe, and tongue, and people, and nation," 5:9.

To "ransom" means specifically to buy back, to deliver by means of purchase; and the kindred expression, to "redeem," means to deliver by payment of a ransom. We are taught that Christ is our Ransomer, our Redeemer, and that He has purchased our redemption at a tremendous cost, the price being His own life. The one pre-eminent service which Jesus came into the world to perform was that of *dying*—giving His life a ransom in behalf of others who themselves deserved to die, in order that they might not have to die. No person can understand the purpose and meaning of the incarnation and crucifixion of Christ until he grasps this central truth, that Jesus came into the world to give Himself a ransom for others. The numerous Scripture references to redemption or to the payment of a ransom invariably imply that redemption has cost something, indeed, that it has cost much. The inability of man to redeem himself or any other man turns precisely on his inability to pay the price which the commission of sin has made mandatory. Christ, and Christ alone, was able to pay the price which would free His people from the curse of sin.

The meaning of the ransom terminology as used in Scripture is set forth by Dr. Benjamin B. Warfield in the following paragraph: "*Lutron*, usually in the plural *lutra*, designates an indemnification, a pecuniary compensation, given in exchange for a cessation of rights over a person or even a thing, *ransom*. It is used for the money given to redeem a field, Lev. 25:24—the life of an ox about to be killed, Ex. 21:30—one's own life in arrest of judicial proceedings, Num. 35:31, 32, or of vengeance, Prov. 6:35—the first born over whom God had claims, Num. 3:46, 48, 51; 18:15, etc. It is ordinarily used of the ransom given for redemption from captivity or slavery, Lev. 19:20; Is. 45:13, etc." (Biblical Doctrines, p. 342).

A present day English writer has set forth the implications of the term very clearly in these words: "I do not merely decide that Christ shall be my Lord. He is my Lord, by right. I was a slave of sin and Satan, and, try as I would, I could not obtain my freedom. I was never a free man, 'I was born in sin and shapen in iniquity.' A slave! And there would I be now, were it not that Christ came and 'bought me with a price.' What follows? 'Ye are not your own.' I am still not free! I have been bought by a new Master! I am a slave, the bond-servant of Christ! He is my Lord, for He has bought me. He does not merely 'demand my soul, my life, my all;' He has bought them, they *are* His. I am His, because He is my Lord, because He owns me, because He has bought me with His own precious blood,"[3]

Those Ransomed Must Be Set Free

A ransom, because of its very nature, makes not merely possible but mandatory and certain the release of those for whom it is paid. Justice demands that those for whom it is paid shall be freed from any further obligation. God would be unjust if He demanded the penalty twice over, first from the Substitute and then from the persons themselves. Because of what Christ has done for His people, and because of the covenant that exists between Him and the Father, all of those for whom the ransom was paid must be brought to salvation. Salvation is thus not of works, not through any good deeds

---

3 Dr. D. Martyn Lloyd-Jones.

done by men, but purely of grace. "If we confess our sins, He is faithful and righteous to forgive us our sins, and to cleanse us from all unrighteousness," 1 John 1:9—faithful in keeping His promise that if we turn to Him we shall find forgiveness, and righteous in keeping His covenant with Christ who suffered vicariously for His people and purchased for them the regenerating and sanctifying influences of the Holy Spirit. Those who have been given to Christ by the Father invariably receive these influences and are effectively brought to salvation. Under no conditions can they be called upon to pay the debt a second time, nor can these saving influences be withheld from them, and that specifically for the reason that salvation is by the grace of God and not by the works of men. "Who shall lay anything to the charge of God's elect? It is God that justifieth; who is he that condemneth?" Rom. 8:33, 34. "He that believeth hath eternal life," John 6:47. As God's elect we have the assurance that "neither death, nor life, nor angels, nor principalities, nor things present, nor things to come, nor powers, nor height, nor depth, nor any other creature, shall be able to separate us from the love of God, which is in Christ Jesus our Lord," Rom. 8:38, 39.

A striking illustration and a very clear warning as to what it means to lose the idea of ransoming out of Christianity is afforded in present day German religious life. The so-called "higher criticism," more appropriately called "destructive" or "negative criticism," had its origin in that land. Unfortunately, the language employed in the German translation of the New Testament did not express the idea of ransoming, with the result that there has been a strong tendency to desupernaturalize Christianity and to present it like any other supposedly high grade religion, as merely a religion of deliverance—which deliverance might be accomplished through better morality, enlightenment, altruism, self help, etc. The result is that truly evangelical religion there has been largely dead for three generations; and the leaders of German thought, particularly those in the higher educational circles, turned to humanistic pursuits. "It has been the misfortune of the religious terminology of Germany," said Dr. Warfield a generation ago, "that the words employed by it to represent the great ransoming language of the New Testament are wholly without native implication of purchase... The German *erlosen, Erlosung, Erloser*, contain no native suggestion of purchase whatever; and are without any large secular usage in which such an implication is distinctly conveyed. They mean in themselves just deliver, deliverance, Deliverer, and they are employed nowhere, apart from their religious implication, with any constant involvement of the mode in which the deliverance is effected.... We may speculate as to what might have been the effect on the course of German religious thought if, from the beginning, some exact reproductions of the Greek words built up around the idea of ransom—such as *loskaufen, Loskaufung, Loskaufer*—had been adopted as their representatives on the pages of the German New Testament, and, consequent to that, in the natural expression of the religious thought and feeling of German Christians. But we can scarcely doubt that it has been gravely injurious to it, that, in point of fact, a loose terminology, importing merely deliverance, has taken the place of the more exact Greek terms, in the expression of religious thought and feeling; and thus the German Christians have been habituated to express their conception of Christ's saving act in language which left wholly unnoticed the central fact that it was an act of purchase." (Biblical Doctrines, pp. 388, 390).

VI. THE REPRESENTATIVE PRINCIPLE

We have said that at the beginning of the race Adam stood not only for himself but as the federal head and representative of the entire human race which was to follow, and that Christ in His turn in both His active and passive obedience stood for all of those who were to be saved. This representative principle pervades all Scripture, and is the basis for the doctrine of original sin and for the doctrine of redemption. It was, in fact, only because the race as originally created was so constituted that one person could stand as its official and responsible head that Christ, coming at a later time and basing His work on the same principle, could redeem His people. It is as if God had said, If sin is to enter, let it enter by one man, so that righteousness also may enter by one man.

The Scriptures teach that the race is a unit, a family, descended from a common ancestor, and bound together by blood ties. This is in contrast with the order followed in the creation of the angels, for they were created not as a race but independently of each other and all at the same time. Each angel stood his test personally and individually.

In virtue of the vital unity of the human race it was possible for God at the very beginning to enter into a "covenant of works" with the ancestor of the race, in which he, bearing their nature and acting therefore in precisely the same way they would have acted, stood trial for them. This afforded a wonderful opportunity for Adam to secure for himself and for his posterity an inestimable—we may even say, an infinite—blessing. For it was so arranged that if he stood his probation and rendered the perfect obedience which was required (and thereby proved himself a grateful, law-abiding son who could be trusted), eternal life would have been conferred upon him and them. But if he did not stand his probation, but committed sin, the penalty of eternal death would be inflicted not only upon him but equally upon all of his descendants. That covenant involved the most solemn responsibilities. It was freighted with possibilities for infinite good or evil.

As originally created, man was perfect of his kind, possessing a positive inclination toward virtue, yet fallible. He was perfect as the bud is perfect and capable of developing into the flower, or as the acorn is perfect and capable of developing into the oak tree. He was not created as a machine or automaton, but as a free moral agent who might choose evil and plunge himself and everything connected with him into disaster. It is apparently true, as Dr. Fairbairn has said, that "Moral perfection can be attained, but cannot be created; God can make a being capable of moral action, but not a being with all the fruits of moral action garnered within him." Had Adam chosen good, then, by that very action he would have produced moral goodness, and God would have confirmed him (that is, made permanent his character) in that goodness as He has confirmed the holy angels in heaven in their goodness.

In language which is at once childlike and profound the third chapter of Genesis tells us of the fall of the human race. Man had his most fair and favorable chance there in the Garden of Eden; and with his eyes open and in spite of the clearest warning as to what the consequences would be, he chose evil instead of good. The Scriptures assert, and the experience of the race from that hour to this bears witness to the truth of the assertion, that Adam fell and that all of his descendants are born into that same state of moral depravity into which he fell. But they also teach that because of the organic unity of the race it was possible for Christ to enter into a "Covenant of Redemption" with God the Father whereby He should act for His people in precisely the same capacity as Adam had acted for the race, providing, on the one hand, that the penalty for their sin should be laid on Him, and on the other, that the merits of His sinless life and of His suffering should be set to their account.

That the fall of Adam did involve the fall and ruin of the entire human race, and that by a parallel arrangement the righteousness of Christ is similarly imputed to His people, is made clear by the Apostle Paul when he says: "As through one man sin entered into the world, and death through sin; and so death passed unto all men, for that all sinned.... Death reigned from Adam until Moses, even over them that had not sinned after the likeness of Adam's transgression, who is a figure of Him that was to come.... If by the trespass of the one the many died, much more did the grace of God, and the gift of the grace of the one man, Jesus Christ, abound unto the many.... for if, by the trespass of the one, death reigned through the one; much more shall they that receive the abundance of grace and of the gift of righteousness reign in life as through the one, even Jesus Christ. So then as through one trespass the judgment came unto all men to condemnation; even so through one act of righteousness the free gift came unto all men to justification of life. For as through the one man's disobedience the many were made sinners, even so through the obedience of the one shall the many be made righteous," Rom. 5:12-19. And again, "For as in Adam all die, so also in Christ shall all be made alive," 1 Cor. 15:22. (The meaning here, as the context makes clear, is that as all descended from Adam partake of his sin and die, so also all who by faith are "in Christ" shall be made alive. In the writings of Paul to be "in Christ" means to be vitally connected with Him, to be saved. He repeatedly declares that those who are "in Christ" have been made alive spiritually. Those who are not "in Christ" are still spiritually dead).

In Christian theology there are three separate and distinct acts of imputation. In the first place Adam's sin is imputed to all of us, his children, that is, judicially set to our account so that we are held responsible for it and suffer the consequences of it. This is commonly known as the doctrine of Original Sin. In the second place, and in precisely the same manner, our sin is imputed to Christ so that He suffers the consequences of it. And in the third place Christ's righteousness is imputed to us and secures for us entrance into heaven. We are, of course, no more personally guilty of Adam's sin than Christ is personally guilty of ours, or than we are personally meritorious because of His righteousness. In each case it is a judicial transaction. We receive salvation from Christ in precisely the same way that we receive condemnation and ruin from Adam. In each case the result follows because of the close and official union which exists between the persons involved. To reject any one of these three steps is to reject an essential part of the Christian system.

But while on the basis of the unity of the human race it was possible for man to be redeemed through the work of a substitute, redemption by such means does not seem to have been possible among the fallen angels. We read of "angels that kept not their own principality, but left their proper habitation," and are now "kept in everlasting bonds under darkness unto the judgment of the great day," Jude 6. And the writer of the epistle to the Hebrews, after saying that Christ became incarnate in order that He might perform His redemptive work, adds: "For verily not to angels doth He give help, but He giveth help to the seed of Abraham," 2:16. Since each angel stood his test individually, he is therefore personally and solely responsible for his own condition. But mankind which fell through the act of a representative without personal guilt can be redeemed through the act of a representative without personal merit.

The representative principle is certainly not foreign to our way of life, nor is it difficult to understand. The people of a state act in and through their representatives in the Legislature. If a country has a good president or king, all of the people share the benefits; if a bad president or king, all suffer the consequences. Children are recognized as the rightful and legal heirs of their parents' wealth and good name, and to a considerable extent inherit even their mental and physical characteristics. In a very real sense parents stand representative for, and to a large extent decide the destinies of, their children. If the parents are virtuous, wise and thrifty, the children reap the blessings; if they are immoral, foolish and indolent, the children suffer. In law we have "power of attorney," and the person for whom the attorney acts assumes full legal responsibility for his acts, whether they are beneficial or injurious. In business we have trusteeship. In a thousand ways the well-being of individuals is conditioned by the acts of others, so inwrought is this representative principle in our every day life.

In the following section Dr. Charles Hodge, one of the ablest theologians that America has produced, has given a very clear exposition of this subject:

"This representative principle pervades the whole Scriptures. The imputation of Adam's sin to his posterity is not an isolated fact. It is only an illustration of a general principle which characterizes the dispensations of God from the beginning of the world. God declares

Himself to Moses as one who visits the iniquity of the fathers upon the children, and upon the children's children unto the third and to the fourth generation, Ex. 34:6, 7...The curse pronounced on Canaan fell on his posterity. Esau's selling his birthright shut out his descendants from the covenant of promise. The children of Moab and Ammon were excluded from the congregation of the Lord forever, because their ancestors opposed the Israelites when they came out of Egypt. In the case of Dathan and Abiram, as in that of Achan, 'their wives, and their sons, and their little children' perished for the sins of their parents. God said to Eli that the iniquity of his house should not be purged with sacrifice and offering for ever. To David it was said, 'The sword shall never depart from thy house; because thou hast despised me, and hast taken the wife of Uriah the Hittite to be thy wife.' To the disobedient Gehazi it was said: 'The leprosy of Naaman shall cleave unto thee and unto thy seed forever.' The sin of Jeroboam and of the men of his generation determined the destiny of the ten tribes for all time. The imprecation of the Jews, when they demanded the crucifixion of Christ, 'His blood be on us and on our children,' still weighs down the scattered people of Israel...This principle runs through the whole Scriptures. When God entered into covenant with Abraham, it was not for himself only but for his posterity. They were bound by all the stipulations of the covenant. They shared its promises and its threatenings, and in hundreds of cases the penalty for disobedience came upon those who had no personal part in the transgressions. Children suffered equally with adults in the judgments, whether famine, pestilence, or war, which came upon the people for their sins.... And the Jews to this day are suffering the penalty of the sins of their fathers for their rejection of Him of whom Moses and the prophets spoke. The whole plan of redemption rests on this same principle. Christ is the representative of His people, and on this ground their sins are imputed to Him and His righteousness to them...No man who believes the Bible, can shut his eyes to the fact that it everywhere recognizes the representative character of parents, and that the dispensations of God have from the beginning been founded on the principle that the children bear the iniquities of their fathers. This is one of the reasons which infidels assign for rejecting the divine origin of the Scriptures. But infidelity furnishes no relief. History is as full of this doctrine as the Bible is. The punishment of the felon involves his family in his disgrace and misery. The spendthrift and drunkard entail poverty and wretchedness upon all connected with them. There is no nation now existing on the face of the earth, whose condition for weal or woe is not largely determined by the character and conduct of their ancestors...The idea of the transfer of guilt or of vicarious punishment lies at the foundation of the expiatory offerings under the Old Testament, and of the great atonement under the new dispensation. To bear sin is, in Scriptural language, to bear the penalty of sin. The victim bore the sin of the offerer. Hands were imposed upon the head of the animal about to be slaughtered, to express the transfer of guilt. That animal must be free from all defect or blemish to make it the more apparent that its blood was shed not for its own deficiencies but for the sin of another. All this was symbolical and typical...And this is what the Scriptures teach concerning the atonement of Christ. He bore our sins; He was a curse for us; He suffered the penalty of the law in our stead. All this proceeds on the ground that the sins of one man can be justly, on some adequate ground, imputed to another."[4]

Strange as it may seem, there are many professing Christians in our day who, while readily acknowledging that our salvation comes from Christ, deny that we

---

4 *Systematic Theology*, II, pp. 198-201.

inherit any guilt and corruption from Adam. Such a position is, of course, utterly inconsistent, and can have no other effect than to undermine true Christianity. If we accept the doctrine of salvation through Christ we have no right to deny the supplementary and equally Scriptural doctrine of condemnation and ruin through Adam. Unless we are fallen in Adam there is, in fact, no reason why we should be redeemed through Christ. The federal headship of Christ in the covenant of redemption presupposes the federal headship of Adam in the covenant of works. The latter is the necessary basis for the former, and the work and position of Christ in relation to His people can be understood only when it is seen in its true relation to the work of Adam. The Scriptures teach that the principles upon which sin and misery came upon the race through Adam are identical with those upon which righteousness and blessedness come upon the elect through Christ. False views concerning our relation to Adam and the effect that his work has had upon the entire race must inevitably produce false views concerning our relation to Christ and His work of redemption. These two doctrines are strictly parallel, and must stand or fall together. They cannot be separated without destroying the logical consistency of the Christian system.

VII. THE EXTENT OF THE ATONEMENT

One further important question which presents itself in connection with the doctrine of the atonement is this: Did the death of Christ have special reference to particular individuals who had been given to Him by the Father and who were therefore definitely foreknown as His people; or was it intended for the whole race alike, for every individual without distinction or exception? Or in other words, Was the death of Christ designed to render certain the salvation of particular individuals, or was it designed merely to render possible the salvation of all men? These divergent views have usually been discussed under the terms Calvinism and Arminianism,—Calvinists holding that in the intention and secret purpose of God Christ died only for His people, His elect, and that His death had only an incidental reference to others in so far as they are partakers of common grace, while Arminians hold that He died for all men alike.

In the first place it should be perfectly evident that the atonement, having been worked out by God Himself, is His own personal property and that He is absolutely sovereign in the disposal which He chooses to make of it. No limit can be set to its value; and the way is now wide open for Him to forgive, freely and fully, as many as He chooses to call to Himself through the cleansing and saving power of the Holy Spirit. He may save few, many, or all members of the human race as

He sees fit. That He does not save all is clearly evident both from the teaching of Scripture and from what we see taking place in the world about us. Just why He does not save all when the sacrifice of Christ is in itself objectively sufficient to save all and He has the power to work mightily in the hearts of all so that they would be saved, we are not able to say. But apparently wiser designs and higher purposes are to be served by allowing some to continue in their self-chosen ways of sin and thus exhibit eternally before men and angels what an awful thing is opposition and rebellion against God. We believe, however, that the merciful and benevolent nature of God implies, and that the Scripture clearly teaches, that in the final analysis the great majority of the human race will be found among the saved.

But as relates to the extent of the atonement, the doctrine of the foreknowledge of God is in itself sufficient to prove that in the plan of God Christ died only for those who are actually saved. For does not God have exact foreknowledge of all things? Is not His ability to predict even the details of history thousands of years in advance based on His foreknowledge? That He does have the foreknowledge is admitted by evangelical Arminians as well as by Calvinists. And since He does have this foreknowledge He could not have sent Christ with the intention of saving those who He positively foreknew would be lost. For as Calvin remarks, "Where would have been the consistency of God's calling to Himself such as He knows will never come?" That a man's accomplishments oftentimes do not measure up to his expectations is due to his lack of foresight or to his lack of ability to accomplish what he purposes. But even a man does not expect what he knows will not be accomplished. If he knows, for instance, that out of a group of thirty persons who might be invited to a banquet a certain twenty will accept and ten will not, then, even though he may still make his invitation broad enough to include the thirty, he expects only the twenty, and his work of preparation is done only on their behalf. Or if he is told that in an adjoining room there are ten chests of gold of which he may have as many as he can carry away at one trip, and his carrying capacity is seven, he does not go into the room expecting to carry away all ten. They do but deceive themselves who, admitting God's foreknowledge, say that Christ died for all men; for what is that but to attribute folly to Him whose ways are perfect? To represent God as earnestly striving to do what he knows He will not do is to represent Him as acting foolishly.

In accordance with this obvious truth the Scriptures teach that Christ died specifically for His people; and nowhere do they teach, either directly or by good and necessary inference that He died for all men alike. Those for whom He died are referred to as "His people," "my people," "the sheep," "the church," "many," or other terms which mean less than the entire human race: e.g., "Thou shalt call His name Jesus; for it is He that shall save *His people* from their sins," Matt. 1:21. "He was cut off out of the land of the living for the transgression of *my people* to whom the stroke was due," Is. 53:8. "I lay down my life for *the sheep*," John 10:15. "The Good Shepherd layeth down His life for *the sheep*," John 10:11. To the unbelieving Jews Jesus said, "Ye believe not, because ye are not of *my sheep*," John 10:26. It was *"the church* of the Lord, which he purchased with His own blood," Acts 20:28. "Christ loved *the church* and gave Himself up for it," Eph. 5:25. "He bare the sin of *many*," Is. 53:12. Christ was "once offered to bear the sins of *many*," Heb. 9:28. "I pray not for the world, but for *those whom thou hast given me;* for *they are thine*," John 17:9. The high priest of ancient Israel offered sacrifice, not for the whole world, but only for the penitent children of Israel. And under the symbolism of the bride and the Lamb the book of Revelation portrays Christ's peculiar and electing and discriminating love for His people, 21:2, 9.

Christ's death had special reference to His people is set forth when He is said to have been a *ransom*,—"The Son of man came not to be ministered unto, but to minister, and to give His life a ransom for many," Matt. 20:28. The nature of a ransom is such that when paid and accepted it automatically frees those for whom it was intended. No further obligation can be charged against them. If the death of Christ was a ransom for all men alike, if by His death He purchased all mankind, then the regenerating and cleansing power of the Holy Spirit which He purchased for them must then be communicated not merely to some but to all alike, and the penalty of eternal punishment cannot be justly inflicted on any. If, as we have said, God is so just that He cannot pardon sin without an atonement, He would certainly be most unjust if He demanded the penalty twice over, once from the Substitute and again from the persons themselves.

THE SOVEREIGNTY OF GOD

The notion that God has ever striven to accomplish a purpose and has failed, particularly the notion that He can be defeated by the will of puny man, is contradicted by the strong emphasis that the Scriptures place on the sovereignty of God. To cite only a few examples: "He doeth according to His will in the army of heaven, and among the inhabitants of the earth; and none can stay His hand, or say unto Him, What doest thou?," Dan. 4:35. "Ah Lord Jehovah! behold, thou hast made the heavens and the earth by thy great power and by thine outstretched arm; and there is nothing too hard for thee," Jer. 32:17. "Jehovah of hosts hath sworn, saying, Surely, as I have thought, so shall it come to pass; and as I have purposed, so shall it stand.... For Jehovah of hosts hath purposed, and who shall annul it? and

His hand is stretched out, and who shall turn it back?" Is. 14:24, 27. "I am God, and there is none like me; declaring the end from the beginning, and from ancient times things that are not yet done; saying, My counsel shall stand, and I will do all my pleasure.... I have spoken; I will bring it to pass; I have purposed, I will also do it." Is. 46:9-11. "Is anything too hard for Jehovah?" Gen. 18:14. "I know that thou canst do all things, And that no purpose of thine can be restrained," Job 42:2. "Our God is in the heavens: He hath done whatsoever He pleased," Ps. 115:3. "All authority hath been given unto me [Christ] in heaven and on earth," Matt. 28:18. "And He put all things in subjection under His feet, and gave Him to be head over all things to the church," Eph. 1:22. "In whom also we were made a heritage, having been foreordained according to the purpose of Him who worketh all things after the counsel of His will," Eph. 1:11.

Certainly these verses teach that God is the sovereign Ruler of heaven and earth, that the entire course of events is under His providential control, and that nothing does or can occur except by either His decretive or permissive will. Since the atonement was worked out by God Himself we may rest assured that it is therefore fully adequate to accomplish the purpose for which it was intended. That any particular person fails to be saved by it can be for no other reason than that he was not included in the plan of redemption. For if pardon has been purchased for all, then of necessity all would have been saved; for universal redemption means universal salvation.

In another connection the present writer has said: "Shall we not believe that God can convert a sinner when He pleases? Cannot the Almighty, the omnipotent Ruler of the universe, change the characters of the creatures He has made? He changed the water into wine at Cana, and sovereignly converted Saul on the road to Damascus. The leper said, 'Lord, if thou wilt, thou canst make me clean,' and at a word his leprosy was cleansed. God is as able to cleanse the soul as the body, for He created both. We believe that if He chose to do so He could raise up such a flood of Christian ministers, missionaries and teachers of the Word that the world would be converted in a very short time. If He actually purposed to save all men He could, if He chose, send hosts of angels to instruct them and to do supernatural works on the earth. He could Himself work marvelously on the heart of every person so that no one would be lost. Since evil exists only by His permission and within the bounds that He has set for it, He could, if He chose, blot it completely out of existence. His power was shown in the work of the destroying angel who in one night slew all of the first-born of the Egyptians (Ex. 12:29), and in another night slew 185,000 of the Assyrian army (2 Kings 19:35). It was shown when the earth opened and swallowed Korah and his rebellious allies (Num. 16:31-33). Ananias and Sapphira were smitten (Acts 5:1-11); King Herod was smitten and died a horrible death (Acts 12:23). God has lost none of His power, and it is highly dishonoring to Him to suppose that He is struggling along with the human race doing the best He can but unable to accomplish His purposes. The Arminian idea which assumes that the serious intentions of God may in some cases be defeated, and that man, who is not only a creature but a sinful creature, can exercise veto power over the plans of Almighty God, is in striking contrast with the Biblical idea of His immeasurable greatness and exaltation by which he is removed from all the weakness of humanity. That the plans of men are not always executed is due to a lack of wisdom or of power; but since God is unlimited in these and all other resources, no unforeseen emergencies can arise, and there is never any occasion for a revision of plans. To suppose that His plans fail and that He strives to no effect, is to reduce Him to the level of His creatures."

While we have not space here for an adequate discussion of the Calvinistic doctrine of Election, we must, however, call attention to the fact that the Scriptures teach that from all eternity the Father gave to the Son a people, the elect, an innumerable multitude, for whom the Son on His part met the requirements of justice at the appointed time. There are, of course, some who, either because they are not acquainted with the Scripture, or because they have never given the matter serious study, deny that there has been any such thing as an election at all. They start at the very word as though it were a spectre just come from the shades and never seen before. Yet, in the New Testament alone, the words *ekletos, ekloga,* and *eklego, elect, election, choose,* are found some forty-seven or forty-eight times. Five times in the seventeenth chapter of John Jesus refers to "those given [Him] by the Father." In writing to the saints at Ephesus Paul declares that God "chose us in Him [Christ] before the foundation of the world [that is, in eternity]... having foreordained us unto adoption as sons through Jesus Christ unto Himself, according to the good pleasure of His will," Eph. 1:4, 5. The love which caused God to send Christ into the world to suffer and die was not a general and indiscriminate and ineffectual love of which all persons equally are the objects, but a peculiar, mysterious, infinite love for His elect, His chosen. Any theory which denies this great and precious truth, and which attempts to explain away this redemptive love as general benevolence or philanthropy of which all men alike are the objects, many of whom are allowed to perish, is simply contrary to Scripture.

The Universalistic Passages

There are, of course, a considerable number of Scripture references which are often quoted to prove that Christ died for all men alike. But none of them definitely teach universal redemption. When in Col. 1:28, for example, Paul refers to his work of "admonishing *every man* and teaching *every man* in all wisdom, that we may present *every man* perfect in Christ," he could not have meant that he expected every man in the world to be made perfect in Christ. Evidently the words "every man" refer to those spoken of in the immediate context, namely, to "His saints" mentioned in verse 26, to whom he says God was pleased to reveal these things. When in Heb. 2:9 we read, "That by the grace of God He should taste of death for *every man*," the reference evidently is to those mentioned in the immediate context, the "many sons" in verse 10, of whose salvation He is declared to be the Author. The Bible is written in the language of the common people, and we very naturally and very often use such expressions as "every man," "every one," "all," etc., with an implied limitation. When we read the historic words, "England expects *every man* this day to do his duty," we readily understand that Admiral Nelson had in mind not every man throughout the world, nor even every Englishman, but only those who were about to engage on the side of England in the battle of Trafalgar.

In a number of the supposedly universalistic passages in which "all" or "all men" are mentioned, the reference is not to all men individually, but to "all kinds of men," Jews and Gentiles, without reference to nationality, color, or social position, and to women and children as well. In some fifty places throughout the New Testament the words "all" and "every" are used in a limited sense, e.g.: "Ye shall be hated of *all* men for my name's sake," Matt. 10:22. "*All* hold John as a prophet," Matt. 21:26. "There went out a decree from Caesar Augustus, that *all the world* should be enrolled... and *all* went to enroll themselves, *every one* to his own city," Luke 2:1-3. "*All* men reasoned in their hearts concerning John," Luke 3:15, "Woe unto you, when *all* men shall speak well of you," Luke 6:26. "If we let Him thus alone, *all men* will believe on Him," John 11:48. "And they sold their possessions and goods, and parted them to *all*, according as *any man* had need," Acts 2:45. "My manner of life then from my youth up, know *all* the Jews," Acts 26:4. "We are our epistle, written in our hearts, known and read of *all* men," 2 Cor. 3:2. When Jesus said that "Every sin and blasphemy shall be forgiven unto men; but the blasphemy against the Spirit shall not be forgiven," Matt. 12:31, He evidently meant that all kinds of sin when repented of, except blasphemy against the Holy Spirit (which is not repented of), would be forgiven.

In not one of the foregoing instances does the word "all" mean all men without exception living on the earth at the time the words were spoken, much less does it mean all who had lived in the past, together with all who were to live in the future. Clearly the doctrine of universal redemption cannot be based on the words "all" or "every" or the phrase "all men."

Nor does John 3:16 teach universal redemption as is so generally assumed, — "For God so loved the world, that He gave His only begotten Son, that whosoever believeth on Him should not perish, but have eternal life." In the first place this verse teaches that the redemption which the Jews thought to monopolize is universal as to space. God so loved the *world*, not just a little portion of it, nor one small nation, but the world as a whole, Jews and Gentiles, white and colored, brown and yellow, rich and poor, free and slave, that He gave His only begotten Son for its redemption. And not only the extensity, but the intensity of God's love is made plain by the little word "so," — God *so* loved he world, that He gave His only begotten Son to die for it. Moreover it is the world that is to be redeemed or Christianized. While numerous individuals are lost, in the final analysis the great majority of the human race is to be found among the saved. This verse does not say that God gave His Son that *none* should perish, or that *all* should have eternal life, but that those who believe on Him should be saved,—and from other Scripture we learn that only a portion of those who hear the message do believe, and that those believe only because divine grace causes them to believe: "Except one be born anew (marginal reading: born from above), he cannot see the kingdom of God," John 3:3; "No one can come to me, except the Father that sent me draw him," John 6:44. Nowhere does Scripture either directly assert or imply that Christ died in the stead of all men, or with the purpose of saving all men.

The Westminster Confession

Concerning the extent of the atonement and the relative positions of the elect and the non-elect, the Westminster Confession says: "As God hath appointed the elect unto glory, so hath He, by the eternal and most free purpose of His will, foreordained all the means thereunto. Wherefore they who are elected being fallen in Adam, are redeemed by Christ, are effectually called unto faith in Christ by His Spirit working in them in due season; are justified, adopted, sanctified, and kept by His power through faith unto salvation. Neither are any other redeemed by Christ, effectually called, justified, adopted, sanctified, and saved but the elect only." (Ch. III; sec. 6).

This does not mean that any poor sinner who desires salvation is rejected, and the attempt to portray it as doing that is nothing but a gross caricature. All those who sincerely desire salvation will certainly be found among the redeemed. None except the regenerate ever have this desire in the first place. Concerning those in the unregenerate state, the Scriptures declare: "The natural man receiveth not the things of the Spirit of God:

for they are foolishness unto him; and he cannot know them, because they are spiritually judged," 1 Cor. 2:14; "There is none righteous, no, not one; There is none that understandeth. There is none that seeketh after God.... There is none that doeth good, no, not so much as one.... There is no fear of God before their eyes," Rom. 3:10-18; "The word of the cross is to them that perish foolishness, but unto us who are saved it is the power of God," 1 Cor. 1:18; "And this is the judgment, that light is come into the world, and men loved the darkness rather than the light; for their works were evil," John 3:19. On the other hand the Scriptures declare concerning the regenerate: "And you did He make alive, when ye were dead through your trespasses and sins," Eph. 2:1; "If any man is in Christ, he is a new creature," 2 Cor. 5:17; and, "He that heareth my word, and believeth Him that sent me, hath eternal life, and cometh not into judgment, but hath passed out of death into life," John 5:24. We have the unconditional promise of Christ that every one who hungers or thirsts after righteousness "shall be filled," Matt. 5:6. "I will give unto him that is athirst of the fountain of the water of life freely," He declares in Rev. 21:6; and in Rev. 22:17 He again says that "he that will" may "take the water of life freely." It does not detract in the least from these promises when we give God the glory and say that "he that wills" to take the water of life freely has been made willing by a divine operation—that he who thirsts for the water of life has been made thirsty by the Spirit of God—that those who feel the need of salvation and want deliverance through the great Ransom have been made, by sovereign grace and the regenerating power of the Holy Spirit, to feel their need and to desire this great deliverance.

THE ATONEMENT UNLIMITED IN VALUE AND POWER

When we speak of the atonement as "limited" we do not mean that any limit can be set to its value or power. Its value is determined by the dignity of the person making it; and since Christ suffered as a Divine-human person the value of His atonement is infinite. It is *sufficient* for the salvation of the entire race, and might have saved every member of the race if that had been God's plan; but it is *efficient* only for those to whom it is applied by the Holy Spirit. It is limited only in the sense that it was intended for, and is applied to, particular persons, namely, for and to those who actually are saved. It is indifferently as well adapted to the salvation of one man as to that of another, thus making objectively possible the salvation of all men. But because of subjective difficulties arising out of the inability of fallen men either to see or appreciate the things of God, only those who are regenerated by the Holy Spirit respond to it and are saved. God could change all human hearts by His mighty regenerating and convincing power if He chose to do so. He wrought mightily in the heart of Saul of Tarsus and made him into a new man, as He has wrought mightily in the heart of every other member of this fallen race who has been translated from the kingdom of darkness to the kingdom of light. But for reasons which have not been fully revealed He does not apply this grace to all.

The Gospel is, nevertheless, to be offered to all men, with the assurance that it is exactly adapted to the needs of all men, and that God has decreed that all who place their faith in Christ shall be saved by Him. No man is lost because of any deficiency in the objective atonement, or because God has placed any barrier in His way, but only because of subjective difficulties, specifically, because his own evil disposition and his freely exercised wicked will prevent his believing and accepting that atonement. God's attitude is perhaps best summed up in the parable of the marriage feast and the slighted invitations, where the king sends this message to the invited guests, "I have made ready my dinner;

my oxen and my fatlings are killed, and all things are ready: come to the marriage feast," Matt. 22:4.

In reality Arminians do limit the atonement as certainly as do Calvinists. For while Calvinists limit its *extent* in that they say it is not applied to all persons (although they believe that much the greater portion of the human race will eventually be saved), Arminians limit its *power* or inherent value; for they say that in itself it does not save anybody, that in each individual in order to become effective it must be supplemented by faith and evangelical obedience on the part of the person and that each person is sovereign in determining whether or not he will have faith in Christ. Calvinists limit the atonement quantitatively, but not qualitatively; Arminians limit it qualitatively, but not quantitatively. Calvinists believe in an atonement of high value,—and the emphasis which the Scriptures place on the sovereignty and goodness and holiness of God implies that He will apply it very freely and very widely. Arminians believe in an atonement of wide extension,—an atonement reaching to every individual throughout the entire world, although they are compelled to admit that in many instances its effects are not very potent and that great multitudes, paricularly in heathen lands, give very little if any evidence of its effects. The fact of the matter is that Arminians actually place more severe limitations on the atonement than do Calvinists. For when it is made universal its inherent value is destroyed. If it is applied to all men, and if many nevertheless continue in their lost condition, the only possible conclusion is that in itself it does not actually save anybody. According to the Arminian theory the atonement has simply made it possible for all men to co-operate with divine grace by doing meritorious works and thus secure their own salvation,—if they will. But in that system salvation can no longer be said to be by grace, but by grace plus works. The nature of the atonement settles its extent. If it was merely designed to make salvation possible, it had reference to all men. If it effectively secured salvation, it had reference only to certain people, that is, to the elect. As Dr. Charles Hodge has pointed out, "The sin of Adam did not make the condemnation of all men merely possible; it was the ground of their actual condemnation. So the righteousness of Christ did not make the salvation of men merely possible; it secured the actual salvation of those for whom He wrought." And Dr. Warfield says, "The things we have to choose between are an atonement of high value, or an atonement of wide extension. The two cannot go together." The fact of the matter is that the work of Christ cannot be universalized without destroying its substance.

General Benefits Received Through Common Grace

We do not deny, of course, that all mankind does receive many and important blessings because of the work of Christ. The penalty which would have been inflicted because of sin is temporarily postponed. Fallen man in this world remains on a much higher plane than that of the fallen angels who have been abandoned to evil and who are commonly referred to in Scripture as evil spirits or demons. As the Gospel is preached and the plan of redemption is progressively worked out, mankind at large shares many uplifting influences. The forces of evil are kept within bounds, and incomparably higher standards of moral, social and economic life are maintained. Paul could say to the heathen people of Lystra that God "left not Himself without witness, in that He did good and gave you from heaven rains and fruitful seasons, filling your hearts with food and gladness," Acts 14:17. God makes His sun to shine on the evil and the good, and sends rain on the just and the unjust. These are the blessings of common grace. Though designed primarily for the elect, they are shared by all mankind; and since this world is not the place of final rewards and punishments, but the place of discipline and testing and development for the Lord's people, these blessings are oftentimes enjoyed in greater abundance by the non-elect than by the elect. But in themselves they are not sufficient to bring a single soul to salvation. They are on an entirely different plane from the blessings of special grace, which are regeneration, justification, adoption, sanctification and glorification. But in a secondary way the blessings of common grace are designed to serve God's purpose in revealing His glory, manifesting His character, filling the world with beauty and happiness, and in general playing their necessary part in the development of His kingdom. There is, then, a sense in which Christ died for all men, and we do not reply to the Arminian tenet with an unqualified negative. But what we do maintain is that His death had special reference to the elect, that with the accompanying influences of the Holy Spirit which are secured by it, it is effectual for their salvation, and that the effects which are produced in others are only incidental to this one great purpose.

Moreover, we find that there is marked discrimination between the treatment accorded fallen men and that accorded the fallen angels. For while Christ took upon Himself human nature and provided redemption for fallen men, nothing like that has been done for fallen angels. In the Epistle of the Hebrews we read, "Since then the children are sharers in flesh and blood, He also Himself in like manner partook of the same; that through death He might bring to naught him that had the power of death, that is, the Devil; and might deliver all them who through fear of death were all their lifetime subject to bondage. For verily not to angels doth He give help, but He giveth help to the seed of Abraham" (2:14-16).

If the sacrifice of Christ had been intended to effect the salvation of all men indiscriminately instead of the elect only, then undoubtedly the information concerning it would have been transmitted to all men indiscriminately instead of being withheld from two-thirds of the race even at this late date two thousand years after it was accomplished. It is indeed hard to see in what sense redemption can be said to be general or universal when so many people through all the ages have been left in total ignorance concerning it.

Leaving aside the views of unbelief, there are in the final analysis just two views of the atonement which are held by Christians: the Calvinistic and the Arminian. We have presented the Calvinistic view, and we insist that it alone is consistent with Scripture. It sets forth an atonement which is definite and explicit; and its inevitable corollary is a satisfied, because fully triumphant, Saviour, since His work is effective and all those for whom He died are saved. The Arminian view presents an atonement which is indefinite and intangible; and its inevitable corollary is a disappointed, because defeated Saviour, since a large portion of those on whose behalf He died and for whom He hoped do nevertheless perish. The Calvinistic view was taught by Augustine, Wycliffe, Luther, Calvin, Knox, Jonathan Edwards, Whitfield, Spurgeon, Hodge, Kuyper and Warfield; the opposing view by men who in most cases were good and honorable men but who as theologians possessed only a fraction of their ability and understanding. We acknowledge evangelical Arminianism to be Christian, but we believe that it is not in full harmony with Scripture and that it is a compromise toward naturalism and self-salvation. Let us remember that the "Gospel" etymologically is the *good news* of what God has done to save His people, and not merely *good advice* as to what they should do to save themselves. It is the glad tidings, the evangel, that heaven is ours through Him who loved us and gave Himself for us.[5]

---

5 For a fuller discussion of the doctrine of election and the extent of the atonement, see: "The Reformed Doctine of Predestination," pp. 83-161, by the present writer.

VIII. Old Testament Ritual and Symbolism

Many people, as they look back at the Old Testament period with its elaborate system of sacrifices, offerings, rituals and ceremonies, are puzzled to know the meaning of such things. We must bear in mind, however, that that was an age of symbolism. The Children of Israel had just been released from Egyptian slavery, and, as is usually the case with slaves, very few of them could either read or write. The Egyptians among whom they had lived were much given to the use of ritualism and pageantry in their own religion, and in fact even their writing was pictorial. So, making allowance for their limitations and adapting the manner of His revelation to their capacity to receive, God graciously gave them the Gospel in picture. By elementary and kindergarten methods a visible representation was provided through which the essentials of the way of salvation were kept constantly before their eyes. This was, of course, not the only message given to them, but was supplementary to, and to some extent explanatory of, that which was given orally and sometimes in writing by the prophets.

The priestly and sacrificial system was designed primarily to center the attention of the people on the coming Messiah, and to teach that there was a way of pardon and access to God. Like shadows of coming events, the sacrifices and rituals of the old system shortened up into definiteness of outline, then vanished completely when the full meridian splendor of the Sun of Righteousness appeared. What our fathers saw only dimly and at a distance we now see in broad daylight. The priesthood and the rituals were thus not the essence of the Church, but only its passing form, and were to be observed only until the One whose coming they foretold had accomplished His work. That the blood of bulls and goats had no power to take away sins, and that the animal sacrifices were only types of the perfect sacrifice which later was to be made on man's behalf, was understood by the enlightened Israelite. It was therefore appointed that such sacrifices and rituals should be repeated daily.

In general conformity with this Dr. A. A. Hodge has said: "The sacrifices of bulls and goats were like token-money, as our paper-promises to pay, accepted at their face-value till the day of settlement. But the sacrifice of Christ was the gold which absolutely extinguished all debt by its intrinsic value. Hence, when Christ died, the veil that separated man from God was rent from the top to the bottom by supernatural hands. When the real expiation was finished, the whole symbolical system representing it became *functum officio*, and was abolished. Soon after this, the temple was razed to the ground, and the ritual was rendered forever impossible."[6]

And John Calvin has this to say concerning the temporary and provisional character of the sacrificial system: "What could be more vain and frivolous than for men to offer the fetid stench arising from the fat of cattle, in order to reconcile themselves to God? or to resort to aspersions of water or of blood, to cleanse themselves from pollution? In short, the whole legal worship, if it be considered in itself, and contain no shadows and figures of correspondent truths, will appear perfectly ridiculous...Unless there had been some spiritual design, to which they were directed, the Jews

---

6 *Popular Lectures*, p. 247.

would have labored to no purpose in these observances, as the Gentiles did in their mummeries. Profane men, who have never seriously devoted themselves to the pursuit of piety, have not patience to hear of such various rites; they not only wonder why God should weary His ancient people with such a mass of ceremonies, but they even despise and deride them as puerile and ludicrous. This arises from inattention to the end of the legal figures, from which if these figures be separated, they must be condemned as vain and useless. But the 'pattern,' which is mentioned, shows that God commanded the sacrifices, not with a design to occupy His worshippers in terrestrial exercises, but rather that He might elevate their minds to sublimer objects. This may be likewise evinced by His nature; for as He is a Spirit, He is pleased with none but spiritual worship. Testimonies of this truth may be found in the numerous passages of the Prophets, in which they reprove the stupidity of the Jews for supposing that sacrifices possess any real value in the sight of God. Do they mean to derogate from the law? Not at all; but being true interpreters of it, they designate by this method to direct the eyes of the people to that point from which the multitudes were wandering."[7]

With this background concerning the nature and purpose of the Old Testament sacrifices and rituals we are now ready to ask, What did the ceremonial system of ancient Israel teach concerning the atonement?

Under the Old Testament ritual, atonement for sin was made by the sacrifice of an animal. The animal, whether lamb, bullock or goat, had to be perfect, without spot or blemish of any kind. In the law concerning sacrifices special emphasis was placed on the blood. Concerning it God said: "The life of the flesh is in the blood; and I have given it to you upon the altar to make atonement for your souls: for it is the blood that ma-

---

[7] *The Institutes*, Book II, Ch. 7).

keth atonement by reason of the life," Lev. 17:11. The lesson taught was that the life of an innocent holy thing was given to cover the confessed guilt of the erring one. The person who came bringing an animal to be slain thereby confessed himself deserving of death but made petition that God in His mercy would accept instead the life of this his substitute. Sacrifices were offered daily throughout the year, and the penitent sinner could bring his offering at any time. The fundamental element so eloquently symbolized in this ritual was that the life of a holy thing was given to cover the confessed guilt of erring man.

THE DAY OF ATONEMENT

Once each year, on the day of atonement, a special sin-offering was made for the nation of Israel, and the full doctrine was exhibited more fully than was possible in the individual offering. Two he goats were taken from the congregation. Lots were cast to determine which one was to be put to death. When it was slain some of its blood was carried even into the Holy of Holies and sprinkled over the mercy seat. The other goat was not slain. Instead the high priest placed his hands upon its head, confessed over it the sins of the people, symbolically transferring them to it, and then sent it away by the hand of an attendant into the wilderness or solitary place where it would be lost. This goat was to "bear upon him all their iniquities unto a solitary land," Lev. 16:22. In the death of the first goat, which through no fault of its own poured out its soul unto death and thus paid the prescribed penalty for sin, the people were taught that the penalty for their sin was laid on another, on their legal substitute. The animal actually received what the people deserved, that is, death.

Dr. John D. Davis has pointed out that through the ritual connected with the second goat the people were "taught by symbolical act that their sins have been carried away, and removed from the sight and presence of themselves and of Jehovah who dwells in their midst. The two goats together constituted one sin offering. Two were necessary, because of the physical impossibility of setting forth by one goat the two elements to be exhibited. One object was attained. The life of the holy thing was placed before God, and the sin was thereby removed from the camp God then treated the congregation as without sin; not merely as though He could not see their sin, but as though it were actually removed. It was not only covered and hidden, so that God did not see it; but it was no longer in the camp, it had been removed, never to return. Such was the symbolical teaching. In the full sense, atonement had been secured; the sin was expiated, and the sinner was accepted as righteous."

The idea of vicarious and expiatory sacrifice, or in other words, the doctrine of substitution by blood atonement, is woven into the very warp and woof of both the Old and the New Testament. It is set forth with special clearness in the book of Leviticus and in other parts of the priest's code. It is nowhere contradicted, although the prophets gave repeated warnings that the mere performance of the ceremony without a truly penitent heart could avail nothing to the offerer. The priests, who in reality were only types of the great High Priest who was to come, were not permitted to enter the sanctuary without blood; that the faithful might know that only through the sacrifice of the life of another could their lives be spared. And the well-nigh universal prevalence of sacrifice among heathen as well as Jewish people expressed man's consciousness that sin subjects him to the wrath of God, and that that wrath can be turned away only when amends have been made through the forfeiture of life, either his own or that of his legal substitute.

THE TABERNACLE AND ITS RITUAL

In the structure and ritual of the tabernacle there is revealed a most remarkable symbolism, through which the people were given a clearer understanding of the great redemptive truths of the faith. We get some idea of the importance which God attached to the tabernacle and its ritual from the fact that approximately one-third of the book of Exodus, all of Leviticus, and a considerable part of Numbers is devoted to it. Two-thirds of the account of the events at Sinai are also given to this subject. The tabernacle—and later the temple, which was built on the same plan—was designed to teach God's willingness to dwell with His people, and the condition on which this great blessing can be secured. This method of instruction was similar to that with which the Children of Israel had been familiar in Egypt, where every attribute of Deity was represented by some outward form and where, as we have said, even the writing was pictorial.

As the tabernacle was set up, God was in the Holy of Holies, man is outside of the enclosure, and the way is explained step by step as we go from the door back into the holiest of all, to the ark and the mercy seat and the shekinah light which was the visible presence of God. Here the mystery as to how a holy God can dwell with sinful man, and how sinful man is enabled to come into the presence of a holy God, is solved. The tabernacle was a tent, God's tent, pitched at a considerable distance outside the camp,—about two-thirds of a mile. God called the people to Him. But to get to Him they had to come out from the camp. The corresponding truth is that God dwells in Christ, and to get to Him we have to come out from the "world" with its sinful ways and practices. Christ is our tabernacle,—"And the

Word became flesh, and dwelt [the Greek says, tabernacled] among us, and we beheld His glory, glory as of the only begotten of the Father, full of grace and truth," John 1:14. Speaking of His body Jesus said, "Destroy this temple, and in three days I will raise it up," John 2:19. The body of Christ is the dwelling place of God. In a somewhat analogous manner God dwelt in the tabernacle, and later in the temple; and thus by a picture visible to all the congregation, to young and old alike, to the literate and the illiterate, great spiritual truths were set forth.

The tabernacle, although comparatively small—it was forty-five feet long, fifteen feet wide and fifteen feet high—was a costly structure, worth about $1,500,000. Unlike most costly churches today, it was not encumbered with debt and mortgage, but was provided through the free will offering of the people who gave so generously that there was more than enough and Moses had to say to them, "Stop!"

Surrounding the tabernacle there was an enclosure or court, seventy-five feet wide and one hundred and fifty feet long, enclosed with pillars and curtains. Thus God's dwelling place is separate, holy, shut off from the rest of the world and from sin. At the front of the court (facing eastward) there is an entrance, the only entrance, with a curtain of blue and scarlet and purple, probably symbolical of the heavenly, the earthly, and the kingly. In a peculiar sense God dwelt within the tabernacle in the Holy of Holies, His presence there being symbolized by the shekinah light.

As we pass through the tri-colored door into the sacred enclosure, very near the entrance and directly before us we find a brazen box or altar, seven and a half feet square and four and a half feet high. It is hollow, made of wood and overlaid with brass. At each corner is a projection or horn, to which the animals for sacrifice might be tied. This is the largest and most prominent piece of furniture in the enclosure. It occupies the foremost place and is very important. No priest could enter the tabernacle except he first placed a sacrifice upon this altar, and the high priest could not go into the Holy of Holies until he had placed his sacrifice there. No teaching could be plainer than this: there can be no access of the sinner to God without an atoning sacrifice. Not only the glory within the veil, but the bread and the light and the privileges of the altar of incense or prayer, were closed until the sacrifice was offered. How forcefully it teaches the lesson that before the sinner can taste of the heavenly bread, or see the heavenly light, or pray acceptably, he must be truly repentant and must avail himself of the atonement God has provided in Christ, the Lamb of God! The tabernacle thus declares that God can be approached only through Calvary. And the great underlying doctrine of the New Testament is that we are accepted only through Christ. The fire on the altar was kindled first from heaven, and was never allowed to go out. As the people journeyed from place to place it was carried in a vessel, symbolizing the perpetuity of the atonement. In a ceaseless rotation the morning sacrifice was followed by the evening sacrifice, and the evening by the morning. The altar was the people's meeting place with God. Even the vilest, if truly repentant, was welcome and could present his offering. In the New Testament "he that will" may come; and we have the promise of Christ that "him that cometh to me I will in no wise cast out," John 6:37.

The animal used in sacrifice was domestic—never the wild animals, but those closely associated with men—without blemish, and perfect of its kind. It was not the sinner's gift—there were other offerings which were presented as gifts—but his representative, his substitute. The man laid his hands on its head and confessed his sin over it, thus signifying the transfer of his guilt to it. It was then slain and its blood sprinkled.

The teaching is very clear that the way to fellowship with God for guilty human beings can be found only through an avenue of death. How effectively it testifies to the sinfulness of sin, its fatal consequences, and the need of atonement before God can be approached! Yet it also testifies that God has provided an atonement, a way back to Himself for all who will accept it.

As we proceed from the altar toward the tabernacle we find the laver midway between the altar and the tabernacle. This bowl-shaped structure was filled with water which was used by the priests to wash their hands and feet before they entered the tabernacle for service. As the altar represented justification putting away sin, or pardon, the laver represents sanctification, or the acquiring of holiness, — "without which no man shall see the Lord," Heb. 12:14; "Who shall ascend into the hill of Jehovah? And who shall stand in His holy place? He that hath clean hands, and a pure heart," Ps. 24:3, 4.

Then we come to the Tabernacle, which was a tent within tents. The outer covering was of badger's skin, a strong, stout leather to turn off the rain; the next, of goat's hair, a cloth of which all tents in the east are made; then a ram's skin covering dyed red; and underneath this covering of beauty was the tabernacle, divided into two parts, the holy place and the Holy of Holies, with its ceiling of blue and its walls of purple and scarlet. As we enter the tent we find a single curtain the type of Christ, who is the door. Inside, we find three articles of furniture. On the left hand side is the golden candlestick, with its seven branches, the only source of light since the tabernacle had no windows, and typifying Christ who is the light of the world, the only spiritual light in this world of darkness. On the right hand side stood the table of shewbread, or bread of the presence, as it was called, a table of gold, holding twelve loaves, one for each of the tribes, and representing the communion and fellowship of the soul in the worship of God, just as we have fellowship with our neighbor when we enter his house and sit down as his guest at his table and eat with him,—the bread being a type of Christ, the bread that came down from heaven, upon whom our souls feed and find life, who says, "I am the bread of life." And midway between the candlestick and the table of shewbread stood the altar of incense, a gold-covered box, made of thornwood, with a golden bowl at the top containing the incense which was compounded of four sweet herbs which when burned gave forth a perfumed smoke that was pleasant to inhale, and which was a type of the merits of Christ, upon which our prayers are borne up acceptably before God. The formula for compounding this incense was originally given by God, and any attempt on the part of private individuals to make incense like it was a capital offense. It thus symbolized that nothing but the merits of Christ will avail for our salvation, and that for us to trust to our own good works, or to anything else except Christ's blood and righteousness, is offensive to God and brings death to the soul.

Now we come to the last room in the tabernacle, the Holy of Holies, God's dwelling place among men. It was a cube, which is a symbol of perfection, fifteen feet long, wide, and high. In the description of heaven given in the book of Revelation the city lies four square. This room had no windows, no candle, no light, yet it was the one place in all the world where there was no darkness. For the glory of God shone continually from above the mercy seat,—and of heaven we read, "The city hath no need of the sun, neither of the moon, to shine upon it; for the glory of God did lighten it, and the lamp thereof is the Lamb...for there shall be no night there," Rev. 21:23-25. Into this room no one was ever permitted to enter except the high priest, and he but once a year, and then only after the most solemn service on the day of atonement.

In the Holy of Holies there was but one article of furniture—the ark. This was a small, gold-covered box, forty-five inches long, twenty-seven inches wide, and twenty-seven inches high, with perhaps more resemblance to a cedar chest without a top than to anything else with which we are familiar. In it were kept the two tablets of stone on which were written the Law, that is, the Ten Commandments. Over the ark was the mercy seat, a cover of solid gold, forty-five inches long and twenty-seven inches wide, at each end of which was a golden cherub, facing each other and covering the mercy seat with their wings. These symbolized the presence and unapproachableness of God. The mercy seat was the only seat in the tabernacle, and it was God's seat, the throne of God. It was over the law, thus symbolizing that God's kingdom is founded on holiness. On the day of atonement the high priest took the blood from the sacrifice and sprinkled it seven times over the mercy seat, thus covering or blotting out the law, thereby making atonement first for himself and then for the people. (See Leviticus, Chapter 16). "When God looked down toward His law," says Dr. A. A. Hodge, "on which rests His throne, and which called for the execution of the penalty upon every transgression, His eye rested first on the covering bearing the sacrificial blood; the sins were therefore covered, and God was reconciled." By that ritual we are taught that we can draw near to God, not by our own good works in keeping the law, but only through mercy which forgives the transgressions of the law. Yet while we cannot gain access to God through any righteousness of our own, we must have a hungering and thirsting after righteousness. Had the tables of the law been placed at the threshold instead of in the innermost shrine, we might have thought that we could gain access to God by keeping the law. As actually arranged the teaching is not "keep the law and God will let you in," but "come in and God will give you grace to keep the law." The New Testament statement of the same truth is: "By grace have ye been saved through faith; and that not of yourselves, it is the gift of God; not of works, that no man should glory. For we are His workmanship, created in Christ Jesus for good works, which God afore prepared that we should walk in them," Eph. 2:8-10.

Separating the holy place from the Holy of Holies there was hung, according to the directions given Moses, "a veil of blue, and purple, and scarlet, and fine twined linen; with cherubim the work of the skilful workman," Ex. 26:31. This veil typified the human nature of Christ, adorned with excellent gifts and graces, by which He opened a way for us into heaven, so that Paul says we "have boldness to enter into the holy place by the blood of Jesus, by the way which He dedicated for us, a new and living way, through the veil, that is to say, His flesh," Heb. 10:19, 20. When Christ died on the cross "the veil of the temple was rent in two from the top to the bottom," Matt. 27:51, signifying that God was leaving His temple, and that all legal and ceremonial worship was at an end.

We must notice one more very remarkable phenomenon in the tabernacle: the furniture is arranged in the shape of a cross. The brazen altar is the base, the laver is the stem, the table of shewbread is the right arm, the candlestick is the left arm, the altar of incense is at the center where the shoulders touch, and the ark is the head. This design was hidden by the veil until the hour when Christ died, at which time the rending of the veil, not by human hands but by God himself, laid open the Holy of Holies. Then, standing at the brazen altar and looking toward the ark, the cross stood out clear and distinct.

Thus in the structure and ritual of the tabernacle there is presented the Gospel in picture. The brazen altar, representing Calvary, is at the very entrance; and the blood from this is sprinkled on all things back to the mercy-seat. As the worshipper passes along this wondrous path he beholds the name of Jesus stamped on all he meets. This was the visible representation kept before the people from the time of Moses until the death of Christ. And Christ Himself during His early career, while recognizing the temporary and provisional character of the ceremonial law, rendered it unfailing obedience; for it was abrogated only by His death. The rituals and ceremonies were like the moon shining in the night, not with their own but with reflected or borrowed light, foreshowing the Sun of Righteousness which was soon to appear. And when the reality appeared and accomplished the work to which the types and ceremonies of Judaism had pointed, these latter disappeared, as the petals fall away when the fruit appears, or as the moon and stars fade out when the sun arises.

CHRIST THE FULFILLMENT OF OLD TESTAMENT RITUAL

To us who are privileged to study the Old Testament in the light of the New it is abundantly clear that Christ was the reality toward which the types and rituals pointed. So overwhelming is the evidence that such is usually acknowledged to be the case, even by those who reject its validity. Christ is everywhere presented as our sacrifice. The Old Testament saints looked forward to the same sacrifice as that to which we look back. Their whole system was a build-up for the coming Messiah. Dr. A. H. Strong has observed that "Just as gravitation kept the universe stable, long before it was discovered by man, so the atonement of Christ was inuring to the salvation of men long before they suspected its existence. This light had been shining throughout the ages, but 'the darkness apprehended it not'" (John 1:5). The trail of sacrificial blood that appears just outside the gates of Eden leads unerringly to the cross of Calvary, where "once at the end of the ages hath He been manifested to put away sin by the sacrifice of Himself," Heb. 9:26. In that transaction Christ was at one and the same time the sacrifice and the Priest who offered it. We personally had nothing to offer and no hand or part in the offering—we simply stand aside under guilt and condemnation, helpless and hopeless. Hence the Scriptures declare that "While we were yet weak, in due season Christ died for the ungodly," Rom. 5:6; and again, "While we were enemies, we were reconciled to God through the death of His Son," Rom. 5:10.

We have said that Christ was a priest, specifically, that He was our great High Priest. A priest is one who represents man before the throne of God, one who is able to make a sacrifice to God on man's behalf and who on the basis of that sacrifice can intercede for man. A prophet, by way of distinction, is God's representative, God's spokesman, to man. Christ exercised, of course, not only the office of priest, but also those of prophet and king. Such an arrangement is necessary because sinful man cannot himself come into the presence of God. The Old Testament priests, particularly the high priests, were appointed to serve until the coming of the true Priest. These, however, were not real priests, but only types or shadows of the One who was to come. Christ alone has the qualifications of a real Priest, and is able to mediate with God. And with His coming and the accomplishment of His work the Levitical priesthood, together with all of its sacrifices and rituals, was forever abolished. What they typified, He actually was; and what their sacrifices pointed forward to, He actually accomplished. We look to Christ alone as our true Priest. We therefore reject all merely human and earthly priests, whether in the Roman Catholic Church or in heathen religions, and look upon their continued practice as simply an attempt to usurp divine authority.

That Christ does exercise this office as Priest is the clear teaching of Scripture. "Christ having come a high priest...not through the blood of goats and calves, but through His own blood, entered in once for all into the holy place, having obtained eternal redemption," Heb. 9:11, 12. "Wherefore it behooved Him in all things to be made like unto His brethren, that He might become a merciful and faithful high priest in things pertaining to God, to make propitiation for the sins of the people," Heb. 2:17. He is "a priest forever, after the order of Melchizedek," Heb. 5:6. "But He, because He abideth for ever, Hath His priesthood unchangeable. Wherefore also He is able to save to the uttermost them that draw near unto God through Him, seeing He ever liveth to make intercession for them. For such a high priest became us, holy, guileless, undefiled, separated from sinners, and made higher than the heavens; who needeth not daily, like those high priests, to offer up sacrifices, first for his own sins, and then for the sins of the people: for this He did once for all, when He offered up Himself. For the law appointed men high priests, having infirmity; but the word of the oath, which was after the law, appointeth a Son, perfected for evermore," Heb. 7:24-28. When the whole race was shut out from God by its sin, God was pleased to choose the Israelites as a priestly nation, then to appoint Levi as the priestly tribe, then to appoint the family of Levi as the priestly family, and finally, narrowing down the choice still further, to appoint a succession of individuals from this family as a type of the great High Priest, Jesus Christ.

And that the death of Christ was a sacrifice is no less clearly taught. "But now once at the end of the ages hath He been manifested to put away sin by the sacrifice of Himself," Heb. 9:26. "For our passover also hath been sacrificed, even Christ," 1 Cor. 5:7. "Behold the Lamb of God, that taketh away the sin of the world," John 1:29. Christ "gave Himself up for us, an offering and a sacrifice to God for an odor of a sweet smell," Eph. 5:2. In instituting the sacrament of the Lord's Supper, Christ set forth His death in sacramental terms, saying of the bread, "This is my body which is given for you," Luke 22:19; and of the wine, "This is my blood of the covenant, which is poured out for many unto remission of sins," Matt. 26:28. His sacrifice paralleled the sin-offering of ancient Israel: "For the bodies of those beasts whose blood is brought into the holy place by the high priest as an offering for sin, are burned without the camp. Wherefore Jesus also, that He might sanctify the people through His own blood, suffered without the gate," Heb. 13:11, 12. "Christ died for our sins according to the Scriptures," 1 Cor. 15:3. "In whom we have our redemption through His blood," Eph. 1:7.

Even in the Old Testament, in the celebrated prophecy of Isaiah, the vicarious atonement of the coming Messiah is set forth in graphic language: "Surely He hath borne our griefs, and carried our sorrows; yet we did esteem Him stricken, smitten of God, and afflicted. But He was wounded for our transgressions, He was bruised for our iniquities; the chastisement of our peace was upon Him; and with His stripes we are healed. All we like sheep have gone astray; we have turned every one to his own way; and Jehovah hath laid on Him the iniquity of us all.... By oppression and judgment He was taken away; and as for His generation, who among them considered that He was cut off out of the land of the living for the transgression of my people to whom the stroke was due?...Yet it pleased Jehovah to bruise Him; He hath put Him to grief: when thou shalt make His soul an offering for sin, He shall see His seed, He shall prolong His days, and the pleasure of Jehovah shall prosper in His hand. He shall see of the travail of His soul, and shall be satisfied: by the knowledge of Himself shall my righteous Servant justify many; and He shall bear their iniquities.... He bare the sin of many, and made intercession for the transgressors," 53:4-12.

Thus the terms used to describe Christ's death are drawn mainly from the familiar ritual of sacrifice; and from its beginning Christianity, like Judaism, has been a redemptive religion. The Old and the New Testament join together in perfect harmony, the former being prophetic, while the latter is descriptive, of Christ's person and work; and in the development of the Church the transition from the Old to the New was as smooth and natural as is the transition from the bud to the flower. The first century Christians, accustomed as they were to sacrificial worship, could not have understood the Apostles to have taught anything else than that Christ, like the pascal lamb, died in order that their sins might be forgiven and that God might be disposed to look upon them with favor. Add to this the constantly reiterated doctrine that salvation is by grace and not by works and there can be no other reasonable interpretation. But in spite of this the plainest and most unequivocal language, there are some in our day, Unitarians, Modernists, skeptics of different kinds, who, simply because they like something else better and want to claim the support of Jesus for their system, insist on thrusting upon Him some other religion which is essentially different. But taking the New Testament records as our sources of information—and they are almost exclusively the only records which tell anything at all about the person and teaching of Jesus—there can be no doubt that the religion He founded was, in His own mind and in the minds of His closest followers, pre-eminently a redemptive religion.

One of the greatest tragedies of the world has been the inability of the Jews, the very people to whom this glorious revelation was given, to understand the spiritual significance of what they saw. When the veil of the temple was opened it was symbolically taught that God was leaving His temple and that all ceremonial worship was at an end. "Behold, your house is left unto you desolate," said Jesus in anticipation of His death and the end of the old order. Matt. 23:38. In destroying Jesus the Jews not only proved themselves utterly unfit to further administer the things of God, but also (and that without the faintest idea of what they were doing) destroyed the entire Levitical system to which, for commercial and selfish reasons, they were so blindly devoted. The Apostle Paul speaks of the veil of ignorance, blindness and hardness of heart which keeps the Jews from understanding the spiritual sense and meaning of the law, and from seeing that Christ is the end of the law for righteousness to them that believe: "For unto this very day at the reading of the old covenant the same veil remaineth, it not being revealed to them that it is done away in Christ. But unto this day, whensoever Moses is read, a veil lieth upon their heart." And then he adds, "But whensoever it [or, marginal reading: a man] shall turn to the Lord, the veil is taken away," 2 Cor. 3:14, 15. How tragic, indeed, is the calamity which has befallen the Jewish people, the very people who were "entrusted with the oracles of God," Rom. 3:2, "of whom is Christ as concerning the flesh," Rom. 9:5. Would that they could see in Him what the humble and spiritually enlightened Simeon saw, the promised Messiah, "A light for revelation to the Gentiles, And *the glory of thy people Israel*," Luke 2:32.

IX. Erroneous Theories of the Atonement

As might have been expected, this great comprehensive doctrine of the atonement which lies at the very heart of the Gospel has not been allowed to go unchallenged. Numerous "theories of the atonement" have emerged from time to time and have been more or less prominent in the Church. Practically all of these with small variations can be included under three main heads: (1) The Moral Influence Theory; (2) The Governmental Theory; and (3) The Mystical Theory.

The Moral Influence Theory

The most widely held and the most influential of the erroneous theories of the atonement is the moral influence theory. It denies that Christ died to satisfy any principle of divine justice, and holds that His death was designed primarily to impress men with a sense of God's love and thus soften their hearts and lead them to repentance. According to this view the crucifixion was a dramatic exhibition of suffering intended to produce a moral impression in awe-stricken spectators. It represents Christ as suffering for us as a loving father or mother suffers for an ungrateful son or a wayward daughter and with the purpose of moving us so that we will turn and repent. The atonement is then conceived of as directed not toward God, with the purpose of maintaining His justice, but toward man, with the purpose of persuading him to right action. Christ's work on the cross is then made to be an impressive proclamation to the world that God is willing to forgive sin on the sole condition that men turn from it. His suffering and death is explained as merely that of a martyr in the cause of righteousness, and as the natural consequence of His having taken human nature upon Himself. He is then supposed to have shared in the woes and griefs which human living naturally involves, and His suffering was not an atonement or an expiation in any true sense of the word, but a supreme example of self-sacrifice. And we in turn are to be inspired by His example so that we too become willing to bear our crosses and give our lives in the service of some good cause, perhaps even in martyrdom, and thus work out our own salvation.

The moral influence theory holds that while Christ may have had a great influence in persuading us to walk in the way of the cross, the way of service and self-sacrifice, it is after all our walking in it and not Christ's walking it which really saves us. This means that in the final analysis we are saved by our own efforts, not by Christ's blood. Christ is then not our Saviour in any true sense of the word, but only a friend and example; and the world has had as many saviours as it has had good men and women. It is the same old notion that sinful man can save himself. It is basically the religion of naturalism, decked out in new garments and dishonestly making use of Christian terminology.

This theory rests on the assumption that God is love and only love; and, holding that repentance is the only requirement for forgiveness, it denies the existence of any law which demands that sin shall receive its just punishment. This is really the root of the whole modern assault upon the doctrine of the atonement. Dr. Warfield has very effectively analyzed and exposed this one-sided emphasis on the attribute of love, and we can do no better than to quote his words:

"In the attempt to give effect to the conception of indiscriminate and undiscriminating love as the basal fact of religion, the entire Biblical teaching as to atonement has been ruthlessly torn up. If God is love and nothing but love, what possible need can there be of an atonement?...Well, certainly, God *is* love. But it does not in the least follow that He is nothing but love. God *is* Love: but Love is not God and the formula 'Love' must therefore ever be inadequate to express God. It may well be—for us sinners, lost in our sin and misery but for it, it must be—the crowning revelation of Christianity that God is love. But it is not from the Christian revelation that we have learned to think of God as nothing but love. That God is the Father of all men in a true and important sense, we should not doubt. But the indiscriminate benevolencism which has taken captive so much of religious thinking of our time is a conception not native to Christianity, but of distinctly heathen quality. As one reads the pages of popular religious literature, teeming as it is with ill-considered assertions of the general Fatherhood of God, he has an odd feeling of transportation back into the atmosphere of, say, the decadent heathenism of the fourth and fifth centuries when the gods were dying, and there was left to those who would fain cling to the old ways little beyond a somewhat saddened sense of the *benignitas numinis*. The *benignitas numinis!* How studded the pages of those genial old heathen are with the expression; how suffused their repressed life is with the conviction that the kind Deity that dwells above will surely not be hard on men toiling here below! How shocked they are at the stern righteousness of the Christian's God, who loomed before their startled eyes as He looms before those of the modern poet in no other light than as 'the hard God that dwelt in Jerusalem'! Surely the Great Divinity is too broadly good to mark the peccadillos of poor puny man; surely they are the objects of His compassionate amusement rather than of His fierce reprobation. Like Omar Khayyam's pot, they were convinced, before all things, of their Maker that 'He's a good fellow and 'twill all be well.

"The query cannot help rising to the surface of our minds whether our modern indiscriminate benevolencism goes much deeper than this. Does all this one-sided proclamation of the universal Fatherhood of God import much more than the heathen *benignitas numinis*? When we take those blessed words, 'God is Love,' upon our lips, are we sure we mean to express much more than that we do not wish to believe that God will hold man to any real account for his sin? Are we, in a word, in these modern days, so much soaring upward toward a more adequate apprehension of the transcendent truth that God is love, as passionately protesting against being ourselves branded and dealt with as wrath-deserving sinners? Assuredly it is impossible to put anything like their real content into these great words, 'God is Love,' save as they are thrown out against the background of those other conceptions of equal loftiness, 'God is Light,' 'God is Righteousness,' 'God is Holiness,' 'God is a consuming fire.' The love of God cannot be apprehended in its length and breadth and height and depth—all of which pass knowledge—save as it is apprehended as the love of a God who turns from the sight of sin with inexpressible abhorrence, and burns against it with unquenchable indignation. The infinitude of His love would be illustrated not by His lavishing of His favor on sinners without requiring an expiation of sin, but by His—through such holiness and through such righteousness as cannot but cry out with infinite abhorrence and indignation—still loving sinners so greatly that He provides a satisfaction for their sin adequate to these tremendous demands. It is the distinguishing characteristic of Christianity, after all, not that it preaches a God of love, but that it preaches a God of conscience. And a thoroughly conscientious God, we may be sure, is not a God who can deal with sinners as if they were not sinners. In this fact lies, perhaps, the deepest ground of the necessity of an expiatory atonement.

"And it is in this fact also that there lies the deepest ground of the increasing failure of the modern world to appreciate the necessity of an expiatory atonement. Conscientiousness commends itself only to awakened conscience; and in much of recent theologizing conscience does not seem especially active. Nothing, indeed, is more startling in the structure of recent theories of atonement, than the apparently vanishing sense of sin that underlies them. Surely it is only where the sense of the power of sin has profoundly decayed, that men can fancy that they can at will cast it off from them in a 'revolutionary repentance.' Surely it is only where the sense of the heinousness of sin has practically passed away, that man can imagine that the holy and just God can deal with it lightly. If we have not much to be saved from, why, certainly a very little atonement will suffice for our needs. It is, after all, only the sinner that requires a Saviour. But if we are sinners, and in proportion as we know ourselves to be sinners, and appreciate what it means to be sinners, we will cry out for that Saviour who only after He was perfected by suffering could become the Author of salvation"[8]

The advocates of the moral influence theory are never tired of ridiculing the idea that God must be propitiated. They give no hint of the Scripture doctrine of the subjective effects of sin on the human heart by which it is alienated from God and unable to respond to any appeal of right motives however powerful. They see no impassable gulf between the holy God and sinful

---

8 *Studies in Theology*, p. 294 f.

man, and, consequently, they see no reason why satisfaction should be made to divine justice. If, as they say, God is continually reaching out His arms from heaven toward man, and the whole difficulty is in inducing men to permit themselves to be pardoned, why, then, of course, there can be no need for an atonement, and in fact the whole idea of atonement is reduced to absurdity. But the Scriptures teach, on the one hand, that the justice of God must be vindicated, and on the other, that an internal action of the Holy Spirit upon the human heart is necessary before man can comprehend spiritual truth, or repent, and that this gift of the Spirit has been purchased for the believer by the sacrifice of Christ. Paul very explicitly grounds the necessity for the atonement, not in the love of God, but in His righteousness or justice, declaring that the ultimate purpose of the atonement was "that He might be just, and the justifier of him that hath faith in Jesus," Rom. 3:26.

The history of the doctrine of the atonement shows how very difficult it is to maintain belief in the Deity of Christ in connection with the moral influence theory. On the basis of this theory the example of a human Christ who, supposedly, is nearer to us, serves as well or even better than a divine Christ. Most modern books on the atonement refuse to impute to man either the sin of Adam or the righteousness of Christ, and so they logically deny both the fall of the race in Adam and the redemption of the race in Christ. They see in Jesus only a great teacher and friend, and consequently their religion tends downward toward the level of humanism.

The far-reaching effect of the moral influence theory and the thoroughness with which it disrupts the whole Christian system has been well stated by Dr. A. H. Strong, who declares that "logically it necessitates a curtailment or surrender of every other characteristic doctrine of Christianity—Inspiration, sin, the Deity of Christ, justification, regeneration, and eternal retribution. It requires surrender of inspiration; for the idea of vicarious and expiatory sacrifice is woven into the very warp and woof of the Old and New Testaments. It requires an abandonment of the Scripture doctrine of sin; for in it all ideas of sin as perversion of nature rendering the sinner unable to save himself, and an objective guilt demanding satisfaction to the divine holiness, is denied. It requires us to give up the Deity of Christ; for if sin is a slight evil, and man can save himself from its penalty and power, then there is no longer need of infinite suffering or an infinite Saviour, and a human Christ is as good as a divine. It requires us to give up the Scripture doctrine of justification, as God's act of declaring the sinner just in the eyes of the law, solely on account of the righteousness and death of Christ to whom he is united by faith; for it cannot permit the counting to man of any other righteousness than his own. It requires a denial of the doctrine of regeneration; for this is no longer the work of God, but the work of the sinner; it is no longer a change of the affections below consciousness, but a self-reforming volition of the sinner himself. It requires a denial of eternal retribution; for this is no longer appropriate to finite transgression of arbitrary law, and to superficial sinning that does not involve [a change in the moral] nature."[9]

We readily acknowledge that the surpassing love of God as displayed in the death of Christ on the cross should cause men to forsake their sin and return to God; but the fact of the matter is that this kind of an appeal does not and cannot touch the unregenerate heart. The experience of New England Unitarianism and of present day Modernism makes it perfectly clear that the moral influence theory of the atonement is morally powerless,—and that for the reason that it puts man back on the plane of the so-called natural religions. It takes from Christ His own garment (the garment which

---

[9] *Systematic Theology*, p. 730.

the writer of the book of Revelation says is "sprinkled with blood," which has inscribed on it His name, "King of Kings and Lord of Lords," 19:13, 16), and puts on another, divests Him of His glory, and proceeds to proclaim, not the Gospel of the New Testament, but a man-made gospel, which has no power to move sinners to repentance. The convicted sinner knows that he is guilty and polluted, and that he has a debt to be paid to divine justice. And not until he is convinced that Christ has paid that debt for him can he think hopefully of reforming his life.

Furthermore, it should be realized by all that a tragedy gotten up for the transparent purpose of affecting our feelings, having no inherent principle or necessity in itself, necessarily defeats itself and produces only disgust. An unjust punishment is a crime in itself. To hang an innocent man for the good of the community is both a crime and a blunder. Only when the hanging is justified by the ill-desert of the person can it be seen by all the community as either just or necessary.

The moral influence theory furnishes no proper explanation of the suffering and death of Christ, but rather makes absurd if not even criminal His voluntary acceptance of such suffering and death in the very prime of His manhood. Furthermore, if He died simply as a martyr instead of the sin-bearer for His people, it is utterly impossible to explain why in His deepest suffering He was utterly forsaken by the Father.

THE GOVERNMENTAL THEORY

The governmental theory of the atonement holds that because of His absolute sovereignty God is able to relax at will the demands of the law and to forgive men freely without any expiation or sacrifice for sin, but that in order to preserve a fair degree of discipline and respect for law so that men shall not be encouraged to believe that they can commit sin with impunity, He must at the same time give some exhibition of the high estimate which He sets upon the law. The primary purpose in the suffering of Christ then was, not to satisfy any eternal principle of divine justice as the satisfaction view holds, nor to break down man's opposition to God by a manifestation of His love as in the moral influence theory, but to secure man's reformation by inducing in him a horror for sin through the awful spectacle of Christ on the cross. With that spectacle before their eyes men were to be made to understand what a serious thing sin really is, that it will not be allowed to go unpunished, and so induced to maintain respect for divine government even in the face of repeated acts of executive clemency. The governmental theory does not hold that Christ suffered the precise penalty which was originally attached to the law, nor even an equivalent of that penalty, but something much less, which God in His sovereignty is at liberty to accept as a substitute for that penalty. Having given this exhibition of His displeasure with sin, God is now able to offer salvation on much easier terms than those originally announced. Instead of demanding perfect obedience He now demands only faith and a reasonable degree of good works, all of which is, of course, worked out by the person himself. There is, therefore, a vast difference between this theory and the satisfaction view which holds that we are saved solely through the perfect obedience of Christ, which obedience conforms to the high demands which were originally set forth as the condition of salvation.

The element of truth in the governmental theory is that the death of Christ actually is a warning that sin shall not be allowed to go unpunished, and that the orderly government of the universe can continue only as men do have respect for law. But we hold that the primary object of punishment is not to instill devotion to the idea of government, or to an abstract idea of law, but the satisfaction of divine justice, and that righteousness must be done for its own sake, because it is right. No deeply convicted sinner feels that his controversy is with government or law as such, but that he is confronted with an intensely personal problem, that he is polluted and undone, and in antagonism to the purity of a personal God,—"Against thee, thee only, have I sinned," said the truly penitent David when he saw his sin in its true light, Ps. 51:4; and the humble publican cried out, "God, be thou merciful to me a sinner," Luke 18:13.

The governmental theory makes no provision for, and in fact it denies the possibility of, the imputation of the sinner's guilt to Christ or of Christ's righteousness to us. It therefore represents God as unjust in that He punishes an innocent person merely for the sake of the impression that it will make on others. Ill-desert must always go before punishment. Unless the punishment is right and just in itself it can work no good to society. This theory fails to recognize the extreme heinousness of sin, and assumes that sin can be adequately punished with a penalty less than that which God Himself originally set against it. But if that is true and if God in His sovereignty is at liberty to assign whatever value He pleases to every created thing presented to Him, then the blood of bulls and goats could just as well have taken away sins,—the sufferings of Christ were superfluous, and He died in vain. This theory assumes that man has the power to change his moral nature at will and that to accomplish this he needs only to be surrounded by good influences, whereas the Scriptures teach that he needs a complete change of nature, or regeneration, which benefit was purchased for him by Christ and can be made effective only through the power of the Holy Spirit. And finally, the light view of sin which this theory holds fails utterly to show forth the deep love of God for His people; for it has no adequate understanding of the cost involved when God Himself—not a mere man, but God Himself in the person of Christ—took our place on the accursed tree.

The governmental theory is, of course, an inconsistent and unstable theory, and it is held by only a comparatively small number of people. It was invented by a prominent Dutch theologian and jurist of the seventeenth century, Hugo Grotius, who approached the subject from the judicial standpoint. He held that in the forgiveness of sin God is to be regarded primarily as a moral governor or ruler who must act, not according to His emotions or desires, but with a view to the best interests of all of those under His authority. The work of Christ was thus conceived of as purely didactic, and the cross was but a symbol, designed to teach, by way of example, God's hatred for sin.

The governmental theory is sometimes called the "intermediate view." It is not as seriously in error as is the moral influence theory, which conceives of the whole purpose of the atonement as designed to influence man, while this theory acknowledges that it is in part directed toward God in that it is designed to maintain respect for His law. But in principle the two are not essentially different, for each denies any necessity of satisfying divine justice and each holds that the primary design of the cross was to produce an effect in man.

THE MYSTICAL THEORY

There is one more theory that we must mention, generally known as the "mystical theory." In this theory the human race is looked upon as a mass or unit or organism rather than as individuals, and the seeds of death and corruption which were introduced into the race through the sin of Adam are counteracted and overcome by the principles of life and immortality which Christ is supposed to have introduced into the race through His incarnation. Redemption is regarded as having been accomplished not by anything that Christ taught or did, but by the incarnation in which Deity was infused into or united with humanity. According to some advocates of this theory, in the incarnation, Christ assumed human nature as He found it, that is, fallen human nature, and not only kept it from sinning but purified it by the power of His own divine nature; and men are saved as, by faith, they become partakers of this purified humanity. According to others, the original depravity which the race inherited from Adam was supposed to have been gradually overcome during the earthly life of Jesus until at the time of His death human nature was restored to its original glory and fellowship with God. According to some, humanity is finally to be deified. Redemption is thus conceived of as terminating physically on man in that the transforming essence of Deity was put into the mass of humanity as leaven into a lump of dough. Christ is regarded as having taken into union with Himself not a real and separate human body and soul, but humanity as a generic substance; and the result was a blood brotherhood in which Christ's inner spiritual life was communicated to man, awakening in him the dormant God-consciousness and enabling him to overcome the sensuous world-consciousness.

The mystical theory has never been held by a large number of people, although it has persisted since the early Greek Fathers and has been held by widely separated groups. Its strength lies in the fact that it lays stress on an important truth, namely, the fact that all believers are in a true sense united with Christ and partake of a new nature. But we hold that this union is made effective, not through the incarnation, but through the work of the Holy Spirit, and in individuals rather than in humanity as a mass. This theory is also commendable in that it ascribes redemption to divine grace and emphasizes the importance of holy living.

But there are serious objections against it. In the first place it contradicts the plain teaching of Scripture.

It asserts that Christ's suffering and death form no essential part of His redemptive work, while the Scriptures strongly emphasize His suffering and death as the basis for the remission of sin. Nowhere in Scripture are we told that Christ became incarnate in order that He might infuse divine life into humanity. Rather we are told that He assumed human nature in order that in it He might suffer the penalty which was due to His people and thus free them from the obligation which rested upon them.

The mystical theory is essentially pantheistic in its tendency. Its assertion that divine life was infused into the human in order to purify and lift the human to the divine breaks down the fundamental distinction between God and man, and leaves the way open for a pantheistic interpretation of life. Its logical corollary is that ultimately the entire human race which has lived since the time of Christ will be transformed and restored to holiness and God.

It leaves unexplained the redemption of the saints who died before the time of Christ, since the subjective and somewhat mechanical process through which redemption is supposed to have been accomplished could not have affected them. Some of its advocates have gone so far as to say that there was no salvation before the time of Christ and that all of the patriarchs perished.

In concluding this study we should observe that each of the erroneous views errs by defect. Each substitutes for the chief aim of the atonement one which is subordinate and incidental. But at no time in the history of the Church has any one of these been able to displace the doctrine of "satisfaction," either in the creeds or in the hearts of believers. In the final analysis no one of them makes any provision for the satisfaction of divine justice, and therefore offers nothing that can honestly be called an atonement. The burden of the apostolic preaching was not that Christ's death was designed primarily to move men by a transcendant display of God's love, nor that it was designed to induce respect for some general or abstract principle of law, nor that all mankind was to be reunited to God by some mysterious union of the divine and human, but rather that He "was delivered up for our trespasses and was raised for our justification" (Rom. 4:25). Very few earnest Christians can ever be persuaded to believe that the life and death of Christ was only "a liturgical service, a chant and a dirge, 'to move the world's mind;' a pageant with a moral."[10]

Neither the moral influence nor the governmental nor the mystical theory finds any support in the sacrificial system of ancient Israel. In no instance is there the slightest indication that any Old Testament sacrifice was ever designed to produce a moral influence on the offerer, or to teach a general respect for law or government, or to illustrate the infusion of the divine nature into the human. Always the immediate and primary end sought in sacrifice was *forgiveness*; and the effect is said to be "to make atonement for sin," Lev. 4:20, 26, 31; 6:30; 2 Chr. 29:24.

The fact of the matter is that the satisfaction view sets forth much more profoundly and effectively the elements of truth which each of these theories embraces, while at the same time it refutes and excludes their erroneous elements. In revealing to us the infinite love of God for His people and showing at what great cost our redemption was purchased it far excels the moral influence theory in producing in us the particular moral effect which that theory was designed to produce, while at the same time it avoids the error of assuming that the sufferings of Christ were designed primarily to influence men rather than to satisfy divine justice.

---

10 Charles Hodge, *Essays and Reviews*: Selected from the Princeton Review, Volume 23; Volume 974, p.438.

In revealing to us the true nature of the law of God as a transcript of the divine nature, which therefore is perfect and holy and immutable, it far excels the governmental theory in producing respect for that law, while it avoids the errors of assuming that punishment laid on an innocent person can of itself produce a good reaction in human society. And in revealing to us how we are legally and representatively united with Christ so that our sin and punishment becomes His while His righteousness and inheritance and glory becomes ours, it far excels the mystical theory in portraying the true nature of our union with Him, while it avoids the error of assuming that sinful human nature is cleansed by an infusion of divine life such as that theory supposes to have occurred at the incarnation.

Conclusion

Quite often we hear it said that it makes little difference what "theory" of the atonement we hold. The fact of the matter is that it makes all the difference in the world. If when we contemplate the cross of Christ we see there the eternal Son of God who loved us and gave Himself for us, who assumed the curse and bought us with His own most precious blood, we shall have the supernatural Christian faith which is set forth in the Scriptures. But if in the suffering of Christ we see only a noble example of self-sacrifice which we in turn are to emulate as well as we can and so work out our own salvation, we shall have only a man-made naturalistic religion such as has deluded so many multitudes down through the ages.

With so much of the world in confusion and men's souls so sorely tried as they are today, this certainly is no time to talk of bloodless atonement. The truly penitent soul, conscious of the burden of sin and guilt, cries out for redemption and refuses to be satisfied with anything else. Others may build on the sands of human speculation if they wish. We are convinced that Christ's death is the only means of salvation, and that where it is unknown or neglected or rejected the soul perishes. The distinction is indeed vital. It is the most momentous that can confront any person.

That the doctrine of the atonement has been neglected and obscured in our day is very evident. Only rarely do we hear a sermon or see an article printed on it. Yet it is the very heart of the Christian message and without it the Gospel is powerless. The minister who neglects it either because of a lack of spiritual experience or because of intellectual difficulties associated with it, becomes hesitant and ineffective or eccentric and sensational, — and that for the very simple reason that his message will then be seriously lacking either in spiritual depth or in intellectual background. In either case it cannot be taken seriously by either minister or hearers. No doubt much of the lack of spiritual power and warmth so frequently charged against the religious life of our day is due in large measure to the neglect of this cardinal truth in so many churches. We do not mean to imply that it has been lost from the hearts of the Christian community. For, as Dr. Warfield has said, "It is in terms of the substitutive atonement that the humble Christian everywhere still expresses the grounds of his hope of salvation. It is in its terms that the earnest evangelist everywhere still presses the claims of Christ upon the awakened hearer. It has not even been lost from the forum of theological discussion. It still commands powerful advocates wherever a vital Christianity enters academic circles; and, as a rule, the more profound the thinker the more clear is the note he strikes in its proclamation and defense."[11]

While the satisfaction view was in substance the view held by the Church from the earliest days, it was not analyzed and set forth in systematic form until the

---

11 *Studies in Theology*, p. 287.

eleventh century, when Anselm, Archbishop of Canterbury, set it forth in his epoch-making book, *Cur Deus Homo*. Since that time it has been an essential part of the creeds and doctrines of all Christian churches, Catholic and Protestant.

At the time of the Reformation the Protestant theologians put the strongest emphasis on the doctrine of the atonement. Calvin in particular in his *Insitutes* worked it out broadly in all of its implications. The result was a dynamic and evangelistic faith. A return to that emphasis probably would do more to re-vitalize the Church and to restore its evangelistic zeal than anything else that could possibly be done. The hierarchy of the Roman Catholic Church has been quick to realize that their main hold on the minds and hearts of the plain people through all the centuries has been the Mass, which is the visible re-enactment, by the use of symbols, of the suffering and death of Christ. Even the pagan religions, with their elaborate temple services and systems of sacrifice, are witnesses to the fact that something more than a lovely system of ethics or a winsome example of fine behaviour is needed to lift the burden of sin from the human soul.

The doctrine of the atonement thus emerges as a vital doctrine in the Christian system. On no other basis than that of Christ's redemptive work is any one warranted in calling himself a Christian. In all other systems one's entire relation with Christ, the ground of His acceptance with God and therefore the entire nature of his religious life, is different. The validity of Christianity as a God-given supernatural system of redemption from sin is bound up with the truth or falsity of its distinctive doctrine of the atonement. We are living in a day when many things pass for "Christianity." But Christianity has a fixed and definite doctrinal content as certainly as Mormonism, Mohammedanism, and Christian Science have their fixed and definite doctrinal contents. At a minimum Christianity involves (1) acknowledgment of one's sin; (2) sorrow for that sin; and (3) trust in Christ as one's only Redeemer from sin. The doctrinal content of Christianity has been fixed by Christ, either personally or through His Apostles, and has been unchangeably recorded in the Bible. For any one to call himself a Christian only because it is popular to do so, or because he approves of the general moral or social life that is found in a Christian community, is as dishonest and unethical as it would be for him to call himself a Mormon or a Mohammedan only because he likes certain outward features in one of those systems. We are not at liberty to call anything "Christianity" unless it conforms to the system of doctrine that was established by Christ Himself.

www.ingramcontent.com/pod-product-compliance
Lightning Source LLC
Chambersburg PA
CBHW020123130526
44591CB00032B/467